KIDW

Kidwelly Castle + St Mary's Church

PB 98

Kidwelly Castle and Church
(Photograph courtesy Martyn Jones)

KIDWELLY
– A HISTORY

Legends, Folklore and Traditions

by

ERIC HUGHES

Sketches/Line Drawings:
PETER BURT

Published by the Author

First Impression 1999

Published by Eric Hughes
Cheriton, Greenfield, Kidwelly
Carmarthenshire, SA17 4PS
Telephone: (01554) 890312

ISBN 0 9537478 0 8

Cover photograph:
Martyn Jones

*Printed in Wales by
Dinefwr Press
Rawlings Road, Llandybïe
Carmarthenshire, SA18 3YD*

Contents

Acknowledgements

Many people have helped in the preparation of this book and I would like to thank in particular the following:

Mrs Mary Williams, for patiently typing and retyping the manuscript and for enhancing the text. Mr Peter Burt whose excellent illustrations have brought the book to life. The late W. H. Morris (Town Historian) for his encouragement during my early research and for the vast collection of his papers deposited at Carmarthen Record Office, which have proved of such great assistance. Mr Douglas Davies for reading the proofs and for good advice. Canon William Price for encouragement and timely suggestions. The late Miss Freda Phillips, the late Canon Douglas L. Walters, Mr Joel Gravell, Mrs Margaret Morgan, Mr Howell Gravell, Mr T. B. Gravell, Mr Anthony Lewis, Mrs Enid Harris, Mr John Morgan, Mrs Joy Griffiths, Mr Brian Rees, Mr Kevin Davies, Mr Hywel Rees, Councillor Derek Richards, Col. Kemmis Buckley, Mr Onslow Greville, Rev. M. R. C. Price.

The very helpful staff at Carmarthen Record Office, Carmarthen Borough Library and Llanelli Town Library.

To Messrs Emyr Nicholas and Eddie John and all the staff at Dinefwr Press for their guidance, support and great care given to the final production of this book.

Last but by no means least, my wife Margaret for her support and patience in allowing me to clutter up the home with numerous books, papers and manuscripts.

Foreword

Before starting to write this foreword I asked myself this question: if I was to restrict my reading for the rest of my life to one field, which field would I select? Running thumb and eye over the shelves of my library, I watched go by a brilliant procession of poets, essayists, novelists, dramatists, theologians, philosophers, vagabond travellers and historians. With which of these I asked myself, would I choose to spend the rest of my reading life? I decided on history. In history one finds oneself in the clearing house of all life and all literature; in history one is looking at the backdrop of all existence.

The author of this book would readily agree, I'm sure, that to write a complete and detailed history of Kidwelly would be a lifelong undertaking of painstaking research. The author has however succeeded in writing an exceedingly valuable 'work in progress'. Shakespeare's dictum – 'Much rain wears the marble' underlines the importance of recording and documenting the story for present and future generations before the passage of time washes it away.

Kidwelly is one of the most historic towns in Wales with a dramatic and interesting history and a variety of historic and ancient sites. Its inhabitants have also, from early to modern times, contributed greatly to its colourful character and myriad attributes. Much of this is reflected in the pages that follow. Our thanks and appreciation go to Mr Eric Hughes for his fastidious work in the preparation and presentation of this book.

Dr. Terry James

Introduction

Local history has caught and held my interest as long as I can remember. Here in my home town we have a tale that goes way back into the mists of time, to a period when superstition and legend walked hand in hand. Prior to invasion by the Normans a hamlet of no significant importance was situated here. Kidwelly's real origin lies in its castle, and the borough grew and developed out of the tiny township that emerged around the fortress. It is noteworthy that Kidwelly is one of only three walled towns in the county, the others being Laugharne and Carmarthen.

I have attempted to chronicle the story of Kidwelly from the dark vistas of its celtic past, to its early beginnings with the castle and the priory church, through the turbulent times of the Norman occupation. I have tried to capture the steady growth of the town, its decline, and rebirth subsequent to the industrial revolution, the advent of nonconformist chapels as well as the sporting achievements of the town. I have delved into legends, folklore and traditions associated with the ancient borough and have enjoyed endless hours researching old, dusty manuscripts and books.

To my knowledge there is only one book recalling the history of the town, a memorable effort by local vicar the Rev. D. Daven Jones published almost a century ago and it is well nigh time to update the story. I have made an attempt and trust that others better qualified will follow on in the future. I trust the book will be of interest as I have tried to present it in an easy to read format.

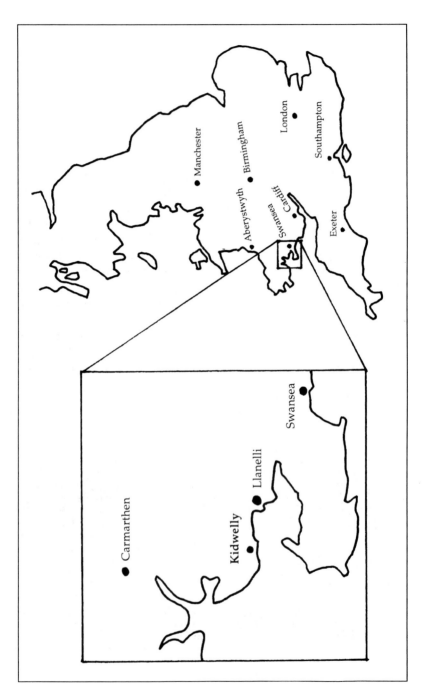

1.

The Town

The name 'Kidwelly' is of great antiquity, far older than the town and castle which came into being in the early 12th century. Its earlier form – 'Cetgueli', is found in the work of a monk called Nennius who was a writer in the 9th century. Cetgueli land was the name applied to the territory between the estuary of the Towy and Loughor, and with it was associated the neighbouring territory of Guhir or Gower. With the emergence of the West Wales Kingdom of Deuheubarth, centred in the Towy Valley, Kidwelly retained its identity and became an administrative subdivision of the kingdom – a commotte. So too did Gower.

Such was its position when the Norman invasion of West Wales began in the early years of the 12th century. It is to the Normans we are indebted for the origin of the castle and the town which

J. H. Davies

Kidwelly, 1759
(Photograph courtesy Author)

developed on the bank of the Gwendraeth Fach River. The pattern of the conquest was far reaching in its effect on the development of the country. The Normans introduced a culture of Continental origin made up of new features – the castle, the town, commerce and trade, large scale farming, parish churches and monasteries, all virtually unknown in preconquest Wales.

The commotte came into the hands of Henry I in 1106 who then granted it to his Chief Minister, Roger Bishop of Salisbury. Almost immediately, Roger set about building his fortress. On completion, the castle had a motte and its bailey or enclosure. The bailey at Kidwelly occupied some 8 acres, and within its restricted confines there developed the town and borough of Kidwelly. Its citizens were foreign settlers – Norman, English, Flemish – encouraged by Roger of Salisbury to settle in the new land as farmers and traders. They were given privileged status as burgesses in the Charter of 1106 by Henry I, which freed them from numerous tolls in connection with trade and commerce in the Middle Ages. They were given specific areas of land on which to build their houses, which were called burgages for which they paid a yearly rental.

Another significant feature was the introduction of a Priory, inhabited by foreign monks of the Benedictine Order, with certainty founded by 1115 on the other side of the river, almost opposite the castle. A small community of foreign settlers, also with the status of burgesses, developed around it and they paid their rents to their overlord, the Prior. Thus, with the twin sites facing each other across the river, the urban nucleus of Kidwelly was established.

Norman occupation of the commotte was confined to its southern part, along the coastal belt. This area became known as the Foreignry or Englishry of the Lordship. Outside it, the wide upland expanse of the commotte was occupied by the main body of the Welsh, carrying on their former way of life in their widely scattered homesteads, pasturing their cattle, goats, sheep and swine, paying their accustomed dues – partly in money or more generally in kind – to the new lord of the castle. They held their lands according to Welsh custom, their local pursuits being conducted in Welsh courts, in which Welsh law was administered as of old.

The existence of this dual community, based on race, was accepted by the Norman. He had no intention of completely disrupting the pattern of native life, for in any case such action would have jeopardised sources of revenue. Furthermore, he was outnumbered by the Welsh. Separation proved to be the most successful option for the governing of two peoples living close together who had widely differing outlooks and customs. In the early centuries there was an uneasy balance which frequently tipped over into open conflict. One of these long ago fought battles continues to be recollected, namely the battle at Maesgwenllian (see 'Legends'). Roger of Salisbury had by now been succeeded in the lordship by Maurice de Londres and it was his forces that fought this battle. The de Londres family ceased with an heiress – Hawise – who married into the de Chaworth family. Payne, the eldest son of this marriage, inherited the lordship in 1268. In that same year Payne de Chaworth obtained a grant from Henry III which allowed the burgesses to hold two weekly markets and an eight-day fair. He was succeeded by his brother Patrick, but the male de Chaworth line, just as the de Londres before them, ceased with an infant daughter. In 1291 the marriage of this young heiress was granted to Edward I's nephew, namely Henry of Lancaster. The lordship and the castle of Kidwelly thus became part of the extensive possessions of the House of Lancaster, later the Duchy of Lancaster, to which it still belongs. It was Henry that began an ambitious building programme designed to improve the town and strengthen the castle and its defences.

The town began to prosper and expand and was now enclosed in walls of great strength. The exact date of completion of the walled town is uncertain but one of the Muddlescwm deeds proves its existence prior to 1332. The town was uplifted in status and rank by the fact that it was now a walled town. Evidence of the expansion and prosperity of the town is the impressive Church of St Mary. Originally the church of the Priory, it was burnt during an attack by the Welsh in the year 1222, but was rebuilt, essentially as it now stands, in the early 14th century.

Entry into the walled town was gained by one of three gates, two of which are still standing. Little trace remains of the walls, apart from a short stretch together with the north gate. Nothing remains of the west gate, whilst the south gate is very imposing.

The town's economic growth had been stimulated by the grant (during the stewardship of the Chaworths) of the right to hold twice weekly markets. This was an important concession as the burgesses had a monopoly of all trade. Although records are sparse, there is evidence of an emerging merchant and ship owning industry trading with France and England. The little walled town began to expand with the introduction of suburbs. There were two areas of

Town Gateway

growth, both governed by the existence of route ways. The first of
these led from the bailey westwards over the hill known as 'Mons
Solomonis' (The Portway) to the Towy and ferry crossing to Llanstephan – the route Gerald of Wales and Archbishop Baldwin must
have taken in 1188 to reach Carmarthen. This development just
beyond the west gate was known as 'Scholand', later corrupted
to Shoe Lane Street and now known as Ferry Road. The same
Muddlescwm deed mentioned earlier refers to 'Boierstrete' later
known as Bower Street and is now the lower end of Water Street.
Where the streets converged and created an open space was the site
of the market cross. The other development ran south to where the
Gwendraeth Fach River had been bridged. The road which spanned
the bridge was known as 'Le Cawsey', now known as Bridge Street.
A cluster of burgages and tenements were constructed here at the
bridge head. It was the start of a gradual extension along the causeway from the bridge in the direction of the other urban nucleus
around the church, and the basis for the lay-out of the town as we
know it today.

   Burning and looting by Welsh attackers disrupted growth in the
town in the early centuries. Glyndŵr's forces led by Henry Dunn
breached the town walls in 1403 but a three-week siege of the castle
was successfully withstood. There was excessive damage to the
town, particularly the 'shire hall' above the south gate. It is a re-
flection of the importance of the town that it should have attracted
the attention of the Glyndŵr rebels. The long lasting effects of the
rebellion resulted in Kidwelly being described in 1443 as being 'waste

and desolate'. Despite the old town being in such a sad state, Kidwelly continued to develop and expand on the other side of the river in the vicinity of St Mary's Parish Church.

The Crown attempted to revive the town's fortunes and induce new townspeople to settle, by granting a charter in the year 1444. This charter, granted by Henry VI was a significant development in the history of the town as it gave the burgesses extensive powers of self government. It brought into existence the Corporation of Kidwelly, the title of Mayor, bailiffs and aldermen of the town, fully capable of holding lands, purchasing tenements, holding its own Hundered Court, and given a monopoly of trade within a five mile radius. It was the first of the Welsh boroughs to receive this important principle of incorporation embodied in a charter. The franchise of the Corporation was said to extend behind the town around the castle precincts, and of this franchise, the Mayor is lord, holding court in the town. The courts for the lordship were held in the castle, and the very first holder of the title 'Mayor of the Borough of Kidwelly' was John Aylward.

The earliest record of the extent of the original limits of the borough of Kidwelly, is mentioned in this charter of 1444, where the bounds of the borough and foreignry, are said to lie within the four

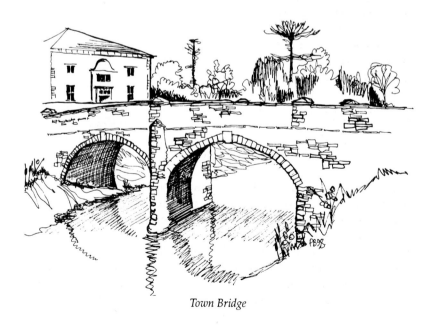

Town Bridge

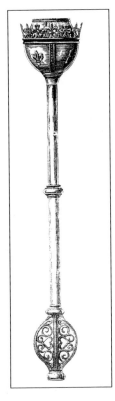

Town Mace
(Photograph: 'A History of Carmarthenshire',
Sir John E. Lloyd, 1939).

Today, the silver maces of the Borough of
Kidwelly are on display at the Welsh
Folk Museum, St Fagans. The pair of
maces which date from about 1610
were deposited in the Museum by
the Corporation of Kidwelly in 1929.

ancient crosses that compose the said town. A survey of the lordship of Kidwelly taken in 1609 relates, "the Jury doth saye that the lyberty and lymytts of the sayd burroughe is and tyme oute of mynde hath been between fowrie ancient crosses standinge as well in the forrenry as Boroughe. In manner following viz – on the west p'te therof one crosse called Treewe Crosse by the lands of Owen Jevan and Audrey Bevan; on the north p'te therof standeth one crosse at a place called Althksanatha; on the east p'te therof the thirde crosse standeth at a place called Clydache; and the fourthe crosse standeth on the south p'te thereof on the south syde of Gwendraeth Favre called Crosse Wyllye". It is regrettable that with the exception of Allt-Cynedda, a hill north of the town, the site of these crosses cannot be identified.

A new town which had overrun the original walled borough, developed on the south bank of the river. Early in the 16th century the town was to be denied the possibility of further expansion by a severe setback over which it could exercise little control. Records will testify the importance of Kidwelly as a sea-faring town from the year 1229 (see 'Industries'). The wide estuary of the two rivers began to silt up with sand and mud, and passage to the town quays became possible only for the smallest vessels. The town, which in the Medieval period had been Carmarthen's rival as a port, gradually lost its shipping trade. On his journey through Wales around 1536 the English traveller, Leyland, described the borough as 'sore and decayed', and further declared that its shipping trade had ceased. The 16th century was a period of stagnation and isolation

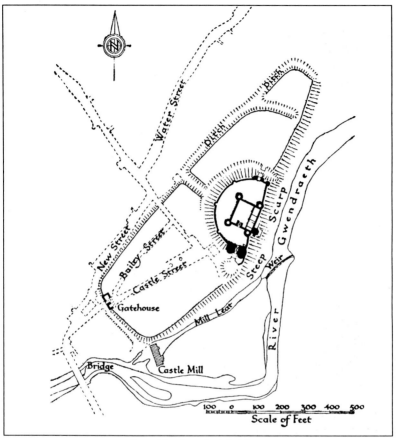

Plan of Castle and Walled Town
(Courtesy 'Kidwelly Castle', C. A. Radleigh Radford, 1933)

for the town. This decline continued through the following century despite further extensive privileges being granted by James I in 1619. This charter granted extensive rights in an attempt to revitalise the town, but there was very little improvement.

Surprisingly, the town was one of the first in Wales to respond to the awakening influences of the 'Industrial Revolution' of the 18th century, with several industries being introduced one after the other. Production of tinplate began as early as 1737 with the construction of a Tinplate Works on the bank of the Gwendraeth River, a mile north of the town. This was the second earliest in the kingdom, whilst an iron works known as the 'Old Forge' was in existence

before the Tin Mills. Anthracite coal was mined on the outskirts of
the town, lime kilns were built, canals created, quays constructed
and the mouth of the Gwendraeth River was dredged. The port
flourished once again as the shipping trade resumed, whilst ship
building was another busy industry in the town. There was a remarkable growth of an import and export trade and the town was
reborn.

This outcome led to an infusion of new blood into the town, and
once again bearing the rank burgess of the borough was considered
to be a great honour. People from all over the country were sworn
in, among them Richard Middleton of Middleton Hall, Peter Chottle
of Barrow-on-Furnace, David Hughes of Penzance and Nathaniel
Morgan of Carmarthen in 1705. William and Nathaniel Dye of
Ilfracombe, Mariners, and Walter Pugh of Bristol, Distillers, in 1728.
Menox Coper of Oxford in 1731, James Darling and Henry Block-
well of Chichester, Merchants, in 1736. William Snow of Plymouth,
William Atkins of Portsmouth, John Thambow of Sunderland and
Charles Owen Teylinger of London in 1771 – the list is endless.
Taking into account that these men paid enrolment fees up to thirty
times higher than those paid by residents of the borough, serves to
highlight the upsurge of interest and commerce in the town.

"The story of Kidwelly had one new and very positive feature in
the 1840s – the coming of the railway," writes M. R. C. Price in *The
Gwendraeth Valleys Railway: Kidwelly to Mynydd y-Garreg*. He continues:

> "Surveyed in 1844 by celebrated engineer Isambard Kingdom
> Brunel, the South Wales Railway was intended to run from a
> junction with the Great Western Railway near Gloucester by
> way of Chepstow, Newport, Cardiff, Bridgend, Neath and
> Swansea. In its initial form, this broad gauge (7ft 0¼ in)
> railway was proposed to run over an inland route from
> Llanelli to Carmarthen across the Gwendraeth Valley but in
> the event it was decided to adopt a cheaper alignment by
> following first the coastline to Kidwelly and Ferryside, and
> then the Towy estuary up to Carmarthen. Work on this section
> began in 1847, but delays arose and it was finally opened on
> 11th October 1852. In its original form, the railway from
> Swansea to Carmarthen comprised a broad gauge single track
> of Barlow rails, crossing the Gwendraeth Fach at Kidwelly by
> a timber bridge with wrought iron lifting sections."

The opening of the South Wales Railway appears to have been instrumental in creating new commercial ideas, with new enterprises being attempted – e.g. silica brick manufacturing and limestone and silica stone quarries were introduced. The quarries were located high up in Mynydd-y-Garreg, north of the town, while two brick works were based in Kidwelly, and another situated near the quarry in Mynydd-y-Garreg. A single track railway was laid to connect Young's brickwork's and lime kilns at Mynydd-y-Garreg to the main line at Kidwelly, and this seems to have been functional around 1879. Despite a 'mountain' of silica rock close at hand and the rail link to the main line, the project had a very chequered history. Meanwhile, the brickworks situated close to the railway station was expanding under the management of Daniel Stephens, and was successful at a time when Young's works were struggling. Later, under the control of Alfred Stephens, the works continued to flourish and at one stage, 18 kilns were in service.

ROYAL CHARTERS

The first Kidwelly Charter was granted by Henry I to Roger, Bishop of Salisbury, lord of Kidwelly Manor between the years 1103 and 1112.

Later, the Charter was confirmed by Henry II to William de Londres, c.1164.

On 28 December 1205 King John granted a Charter to William, son of de Londres. Previous Charter was confirmed by Henry III in 1228.

In the year 1268 a new Charter was granted by Henry III.

In the year 1285 a Charter granted by Edward I.

In the year 1357 a Charter granted by Edward III.

In 1444 a Borough Charter was granted by Henry VI. This Charter provided for incorporation, which in this sense may be regarded as the original Charter of Kidwelly.

In the year 1541 the previous Charter was confirmed by Henry VIII and in 1551 the same Charter was again confirmed by Edward VI.

A Charter granted by James I – July 20th 1619.

This was replaced by the last Kidwelly Charter granted by Queen Victoria in the year 1885.

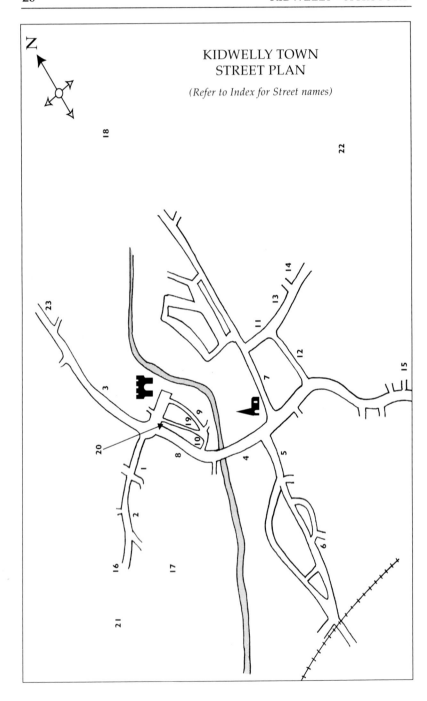

KIDWELLY TOWN
STREET PLAN

(Refer to Index for Street names)

OLD TOWN NAMES

	Present Name	Original Name	Later corrupted to
	Ferry Road –		
1.	(Lower Part)	Scholand	Shoe Lane Street
2.	(Upper Part)	Le Very Wey	Ferry Way
3.	Water Street (Lower Part)	Boierstete	Bower Street
4.	Bridge Street	Le Cawsey	Causey Street
5.	Station Road (Town End)	Vrogmerstrete	Frogmor Street
6.	West Hill	Le Weste Hille	
7.	Lady Street	Seint Mereys Streete	St Mary's Street
8.	New Street	Ditchestreete	Ditch Street
9.	Castle Street	The Baylye	Bailey Street
10.	Bailey Street	Cock Street	
11.	Abbey Street	Longstrete	Lang Street
12.	Alstred Street	Bowmanstrete	Bowman Street
13.	Monksford Street	Monkesford	
14.	Stockwell Lane	Le Stokwell	
15.	Holloway Lane	Le Holwey	
16.	Arlais	Le Arlez	
17.	Cobswell	Le Cobwell	
18.	Gwenllian	Gwenllianis	
19.	Old Castle School (now Community Centre)	Shambles (Butchers, Stalls, Market)	
20.	Baptist Church (Graveyard)	The Great Orchard	
21.	The Portway	Mons Solomonis	
22.	Muddlescwm	Muddlescumbe	
23.	Broomhill	Bronnehill	*(Refer to Street plan).*

PEDIGREE OF THE LORDS OF KIDWELLY

William of London,
Lord of Ogmore, *temp. Hen. I*,
m. Matilda (*Cart. Glouc.* ii, 230)

Maurice of London
At Kidwelly, 1136 (Gir. Camb. vi, 79)
Founder of Ewenny priory, 1141 ? (Clark, *Cartae*, 2265-6)
m. Adeliza

William II (*Liber Niger*, Wilts.)

William III (Clark, 386)
Constable of Carmarthen,
temp. Job.

Thomas (Clark, 451, 573)
m. Eva de Tracy
d. circa 1216

Hawise, *d.* 1274,
m. (1) in 1223, Walter de Breos, *d.* 1234?
(2) in 1243, Patrick de Cadurcis,
d. 1258

Pain de Cadurcis
d. 1279

Patrick II de Cadurcis
m. Isabel Beauchamp,
d. 1283

Maud, *b.* 1282
m. in 1298 Henry of Lancaster,
b. 1281, earl 1324, *d.* 1345

Henry
b. 1299 ?; earl of Derby, 1337,
of Lancaster, 1347; *d.* 1361
m. Isabel, dau. of Henry,
Lord Beaumont

Blanche
b. 1341, *d.* 1369
m. in 1359 John of Gaunt

History of Carmarthenshire
– Sir John E. Lloyd.

Henry IV

2.

The Castle

In the early 12th century the Normans invaded South Wales and occupied a large area of the coastal strip, and wherever they settled a castle was constructed as a stronghold for defence against attacks by the local Welsh chiefs. The commotte came into the hands of Henry I in 1106, and he granted it to his chief administrator Roger Bishop of Salisbury. Almost immediately, Roger set about building his fortress. This first castle was constructed of earth and timber and the site was well and skilfully chosen. It commanded a crossing point of the river near a trackway to Carmarthen, and a natural feature, a cliff above the river was incorporated into the defence. The river, too, offered a line of retreat to the sea, as well as allowing supplies to be brought in if the Welsh forces cut off facilities by land.

Kidwelly Castle, from an old etching
(Photograph courtesy Author)

This early castle was not of a stone structure but of earth. A huge earthen mound encircled by a deep ditch was typical of a Norman castle of this period. On the flat top of the mound a wooden building (a keep) would be constructed protected along the edge of the mound by a palisade of stout stakes. At Kidwelly, where the conquest had to be consolidated, the motte had its bailey or enclosure itself defended with its own earthen rampart and deep ditch, the whole forming an integrated unit of defence. In addition to its function in the defence of the castle, the bailey served other purposes. Buildings necessary to the castle in its role as a fortress were placed within the confines of the bailey – a hall for meals, accommodation for the lord's retainers and garrison, a chapel, stables, storehouses and barns. The first record of the castle is contained in a document of 1115, where there is a reference to the 'hall of the castle'. By 1136 the Lordship of Kidwelly had passed to Maurice de Londres of Ogmore. The castle had a turbulent history in the early centuries and was the venue of open conflict between the Welsh princes and the English kings. The death of the formidable Henry I in 1135 set off a surge of Welsh revolt. One famous battle of this era led to the death of a Welsh princess – Gwenllian (see 'Legends') – and is still talked about in the locality. Her son Rhys ap Gruffudd attacked and burnt the castle in 1159. It was back in Norman hands by 1201, but in the first half of the 13th century it was assaulted and partially destroyed by the Welsh on two more occasions. By 1220 the male line of de Londres had become extinct and Kidwelly passed to an heiress – Lady Hawise. Open conflict continued and during an attack by Llewellyn the Great in 1231 the wooden fortifications were burnt. Lady Hawise married Patrick de Chaworth in 1243 who then reclaimed Kidwelly from the Welsh and carried out improvements to the castle. Their eldest son inherited the lordship in 1268 and it was he who was to adapt and strengthen the fortress of his de Londres ancestors into a far stronger military fortification. In 1275 Payne began a reconstruction of the castle, with stone replacing the timber defences.

The next phase of building took place under Henry of Lancaster who married the Chaworth brother's infant heiress – Maud – in 1298. Henry built a stone curtain wall flanked by towers with a small gatehouse to the north, and at its southern end a massive gatehouse to defend the main entrance and to provide residential quarters. This programme took about ten years to complete, by which time the castle was completely encased in stone and had assumed

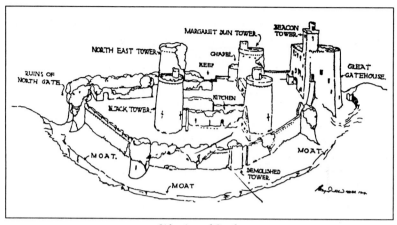

Side view of Castle
(*Photograph: 'An Inventory of Ancient Monuments in Wales', Vol. V, 1917*)

the style it displays today. The castle had been updated as a concentric construction, the basic technique being building defensive walls one within another. This meant that an invader had more than one bailey to conquer before he could move on to the innermost stronghold. The four inner towers and walls were raised so that if the outer defences were taken, the bowmen on the second line of defence could command the lower wall and the bailey. It was not until about 100 years later that the strengthened defences were tested – during the Owen Glyndŵr uprising of 1403. The town walls were breached but the castle withstood the three week siege. Apart from this attack led by Henry Dunn at Kidwelly, the castle does not appear to have played a significant role in the 15th century. The castle was granted by Henry VII to Sir Rhys ap Thomas who carried out further additions but its days as a strategic fortress were already numbered. The castle came into the possession of the Vaughan family in 1630, and was passed by descent to the Earls of Cawdor. In 1927 it passed into state care and is now maintained by CADW Welsh Historical Monuments.

THE LAYOUT

The castle stands on a natural eminence of about 100 feet on the right bank of the Gwendraeth Fach River. Outline plan is semi-circle

Castle Gatehouse

with a steep cliff being a feature of the defence. A moat 20 feet wide
surrounded the castle, butting up to the cliff face

The Gatehouse

The main entrance was the great south gate. Erected early in the
14th century when the original defences were replaced by a curtain
of stone, it was not completed until well into the 15th century. The
magnificent gatehouse is a fortress in itself, with two circular towers
flanking the entrance. A series of obstacles had to be overcome
within the gatehouse before an intruder could reach the interior of
the castle. With archers firing from arrow slits within the towers,
and rocks being dropped down from above the tower, an additional
deterrent was the lowered outer portcullis at the entrance in front of
the heavy wooden door. To get this far the invader would have had
to negotiate the moat, as the great drawbridge would have been
raised. (Chains or ropes were used to raise and lower the drawbridge.) If the enemy passed the portcullis and door, he was faced
with the gate passageway eight feet high and eleven feet long, with

three slits in the ceiling known as murder holes, from which there would have been a cascade of missiles. At the far end of the passage there was another set of doors and an inner portcullis.

The gatehouse provided accommodation for the constable in charge of the castle and was constructed on five levels. On the ground floor was the castle prison with guardrooms on either side. Inside the prison there is a circular entrance to the dungeon, through which prisoners would be lowered, to a bare pit down below. The square tower called 'Beacon' on the north-east angle is a later edition. This is 93 feet high and was probably used as a watch tower – a soldier posted here would have a great view of anyone approaching the castle.

The Inner Ward
Within the outer ward is the square inner ward erected in the 1270s with its four drum towers linked together by curtain walls. The gateways, both north and south were well protected and each had a heavy wooden gate and portcullis. The north-west tower was called the 'Black Tower' and that on the south-west the 'Astregun'. The south-east was the 'Margaret Dun' whilst the north-east tower had no name. The south-west tower ('Astregun') is the only one where

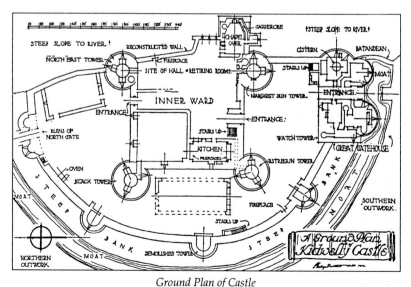

Ground Plan of Castle
(Photograph: 'An Inventory of Ancient Monuments in Wales', Vol. V, 1917)

the floors are still in evidence, as is the dome-shaped roof which is rare and is seen in few other castles. Shortly after 1300 the outer walls were raised again and the walls of the four towers had to be heightened in order to retain the advantages in overseeing activities at lower levels, particularly at times of siege and conflict.

The Chapel

The chapel is situated in a small square tower which projects beyond the east wall overlooking the cliff as part of the inner ward and was constructed c.1300. To quote Professor E. A. Freeman, *Arch. Camb.* – "The castle chapel is a triumph of art, a building amply satisfactory, both in ecclesiastical and architectural points of view, has room found for it in a structure purely military, without in the least interfering with the genuine character of the latter."

The building consists of a basement and ground floor with the chapel itself on the upper floor. Within the chapel to the south of the altar will be seen the double piscina, where the sacred vessels were washed, and a wide sedile, a seat for use of the priest. The beautiful lancet windows and the fine vaulting of the sacristy are excellent specimens of early workmanship. The sacristy was the small room which contained the holy vessels when they were not in use. The room under the sacristy was the priest's bedchamber.

Domestic Buildings

The 13th century domestic buildings occupy the whole of one side of the inner wall. The hall and salon form a long range connecting the two eastern towers overlooking the river. The principal chambers were on the upper floor below which were located probably storerooms with the remains of a kitchen alongside.

Changes undertaken towards the close of the 15th century included the provision of more spacious buildings. On the west side a large hall was erected and a kitchen to serve this new hall. The kitchen, a simple building, had two large fireplaces at each end of the room. Buildings standing against the east, north and west curtains of the outer ward, belong to the same period. The purpose of the first, a large chamber very similar in appearance to the late hall, cannot be determined. The building to the west of the north gate was a bake-house and has a large oven intact. The remaining structure by the south-west tower has two long narrow rooms, one of which was provided with a fireplace.

The North Gatehouse
Little remains of the smaller northern gatehouse which had two flanking towers. On the other side of the ditch stands a masonry pier onto which the drawbridge would have been lowered.

One of the castle governors during the 15th century was Owain, son of Gruffydd ap Nicholas of Dynevor. According to the Bard Lewis Glyn Cothi, he entertained there in lavish style, keeping 3 butchers, 3 cooks and a large retinue of servants.

ROYAL VISITORS

On several occasions the castle of Kidwelly has been graced by visits from reigning monarchs and the first royal visit seems to have been made by King John in 1210.

Edward I paid a visit in 1285 and Richard II visited the town three times in 1386, 1394 and 1398.

Prince Charles, Prince of Wales, visited in 1969.

Other notable people who visited the castle were Archbishop Baldwin and Gerald of Wales (Giraldus Cambrensis).

Duchy of Lancaster – Ministers Accounts – Bundle 573 – A memorandum dated February 22nd Richard II – (1398-99) John Wylkyns, Reeve, answers for "one pipe of wine remaining in the castle after the departure of the late King Richard, and sold by Walter Castell."

Included in the castle accounts relating to King Richard II's visit and stay in the castle in 1398 – probably on his way to Ireland – was recorded the following: "Fuel for Richard late King of England staying for the night in the castle 4 shillings, carriage of fuel 8 shillings, for rushes strewn in the rooms for the king 12 pence."

Today, the castle is the pride of the town, the best preserved of all Carmarthenshire's nine strongholds and one of the most beautiful castles in Wales. The four central towers add great beauty to the structure with its imposing situation, commanding extensive views of the coastline and surrounding countryside.

3

The Priory and Churches

THE PRIORY

When construction of a strong castle was complete the Norman lord would often assign a piece of land to foreign monks who would then found a cell (small priory) close to the fortress, as happened in Kidwelly. A priory of the Benedictine Order was set up by the monks of Sherborne Abbey, Dorset, c.1115, and was served by a prior and two monks. There is no trace of this little priory but no doubt the monks would have conducted services at both the castle and at their own parish church. There was an inseparable link between the Priory and the Church, from the very outset to the Dissolution in 1544, when the monastic Church was permitted to continue its ministry as the Parish Church. John Leyland states in his 16th century *Itinerary*: "In the new Toune is only a Church of our Ladi and by this is the celle of Blake, monkes of Sherborne. There the Prior is patron of Our Ladi Church". When the Priory at Kidwelly was suppressed and fell into the hands of the Crown at the Dissolution in 1544, Henry VIII disposed of it by lease. He granted a 21 year lease to George Asshe and Robert Meyrick, yeomen and purveyors of wine to the king. The following are details of the leased possessions – the site of the priory, all buildings, edifices, granaries, cemeteries, pleasureground, orchards, gardens and fishponds.

The site of the ancient Priory appears to have been on the left bank of the Gwendraeth Fach River, very near to the east boundary wall of the present churchyard. There are many reasons for this assumption – documentary evidence of proceedings at the Prior's Court held at Kidwelly prove that the land now occupied by Lady Street (or as it was known earlier St Mary's Street) was owned by the Prior. In the early part of this century ruins were traced hard by the east boundary wall of the churchyard and this location was believed to be the actual site of the priory, and the land now covered by the gardens attached to the houses in Lady Street was known as 'the priory fields'.

List of Priors

Abraham	Circa 1240
Gervase	1268
Galfridus De Coker	1301
Robert Dunsterr	1346
John Flode	1361
Phillip Morevyle	1399
John De Kedwelly	1404
Robert Fyfhyde	1428
John Shirborne	1482
John Henstridge	1487
John Whitchurch	1520
John Godmyster	1537

The Priors were also rectors of the Parish Church of St Mary.

EARLY CHRISTIAN CHURCHES IN THE PARISH

Many years ago churches were dedicated to St Teilo and St Cadoc in the Parish of Kidwelly and the crude walls of one, namely Capel Teilo (Teilo's Chapel), survived the tide of time and within living memory there is confirmation of its existence. However, there is very little trace of ruins on the site today. The location of the older church is preserved by the name of a district and a farm, Llangadog (the Church of Cadog) and nearby Waungadog (Cadoc's meadow). By a charter held in the Public Record Office, a grant was made by Maurice de Londres of 12 acres of land around the Church of St Cadoc and the adjoining lands of St Mary. This charter is undated, but as it is addressed to David, Bishop of St David's, the transaction must have taken place between the years AD 1148 and 1176 when a David (Fitzgerald) was Bishop of St David's. Most of the ancient churches in Wales were dedicated to Welsh saints; it was after the Norman conquest that many such buildings were dedicated to the Virgin Mary.

Traditionally, it is stated that on the site of Maenllwyd Mawr (see Legends) there stood a church called Llanfihangel (the Church of St Michael). Mr Daniel Gravel of Muddlescwm Farm (on whose land the site is located) confirms that he has discovered foundations of a substantial nature there. A large stone slab was found with a chamfered edge, measuring 7 ft by 15 inches and 7 inches thick, which was transported from the site to the farmstead where it served as a bridge over a brook near the entrance to the farmyard. Its size and appearance would suggest it to be a large window sill. The present whereabout of the slab is unknown.

In all probability the site of the present church of St Mary's was previously occupied by another church. Early documents refer to the church of the territory of Kidwelly, from which it can be concluded that it may have been the mother church of the district. There is no evidence to establish the location of this particular church – we can therefore assume it was a predecessor of the existing parish church having been constructed on the same spot. The assumption of an earlier church accords with the age of the building which now stands, where the style of architecture prohibits an earlier age than the late 13th century. It is also probable that the former church was the one which is claimed to have been burnt down together with the town and religious houses by Prince Llewellyn AD 1222.

ST MARY'S PARISH CHURCH

St Marys Kidwelly   PG98

As the Norman influence spread throughout Wales, churches built of stone replaced the older ones built of timber. The new churches were dedicated to the apostles or to the Virgin Mary and not to local saints as had been the Welsh custom. Kidwelly church had a turbulent early history, as did the castle, and both church and castle were destroyed by Llewellyn the Great early in the thirteenth century. It would seem that the present parish church was erected on the foundation of a previous edifice which probably

The Priory Church of Saint Mary, at Kidwelly

THE SOUTH ELEVATION.

St Mary's Church
(Photograph: 'An Inventory of Ancient Monuments in Wales', Vol. V, 1917)

had been a temporary restoration of the church which is said to have
burnt down together with the town.

The church as it stands now was built about 1320 "hardly more
than two bow shots from the castle" and was closely connected
with the Benedictine Priory. It was conceived on a generous scale,
with its enormous nave, two chapels forming transepts, its tower
and spire. Delicate craftsmanship in stone survives in the window
tracery and the sedilia. Shortly after its completion it received the
gift of a beautiful white alabaster figure of the Virgin and Child of
Italian workmanship. Astonishingly it has survived; during the
Reformation it was taken out of the Church and hidden. Today it is
a feature of the Church and can be found in the Sanctuary. St Mary's
was one of the comparatively few monastic churches which were
preserved at the suppression of monasteries, and was permitted to
remain as the church of the parish. It is dedicated, as might have
been expected under the circumstances, to Mary; such consecrations
became popular under the Norman administration, and are generally to be found in towns under the shadow of Norman castles. In
his book, *History of the Diocese of St David's*, the Venerable Arch-

deacon Bevan described the church: "Kidwelly church may be cited as the best example amongst parochial churches of the decorated style in this diocese, its distinctive features being the large span of the nave, its spacious chancel, short transepts and lofty tower surmounted by a graceful spire". A general look at the church confirms this statement and many authorities also regard it as one of the best of this type of parochial church.

The church has had its share of disasters, the spire having been damaged by lightning on three known occasions – in 1481, 1658 and 1884. The earliest disaster is recorded in the Church Register and chillingly conveys the atmospheric event – "Upon the 29th day of October 1481, the steeple of Kidwelly fell down by lightning and a clap of thunder, between one and two o'clock in the afternoon – From lightning and tempest, from battle and murder, and from sudden death, Good Lord, deliver us". Regarding the disaster of 1658, the extent of the damage is recorded in the churchwardens' reports some twenty years later, and surprisingly repairs had still not been carried out – "The churchwardens of the Parish of Kidwelly at the Archdeacons visitation at Carmarthen on 2nd May 1679 make the following presentment – We present the Church of Kidwelly to be quite destroyed and fallen down since the 24th day of June Anno Domini, 1658. We present the font, bell ropes, and all other things belonging to the said Church to be out of repair. We present the Church coffer is out of repair". John Griffiths, Jenkin Meyricke – Churchwardens.

Sir Gilbert Scott gave a detailed account of the dilapidated state of the present building when he visited Kidwelly in 1854. He made scathing criticism stressing the need for restoration, but for all that nothing was done until the spire was hit by lightning once more and crashed down through the roof in 1884. This disaster proved to be a blessing in disguise because it enforced restoration work along the lines recommended by an architect thirty years earlier. The vicar at that time, the Rev. W. H. Sinnett, organised a restoration fund which resulted in a tremendous response, and he also made a generous personal contribution towards the total expenditure amounting to £1813.18s.1d.

Layout of the Church
The Tower Door dated 1713 (the main entrance door at the time) bears a Latin inscription – 'HAEC EST DOMUS DEI PORTA COELI' – This is the House of God, The Gateway to Heaven.

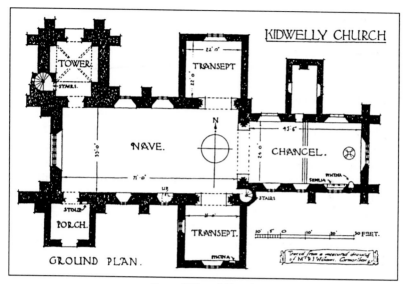

Ground Plan of Church
(Photograph: 'An Inventory of Ancient Monuments in Wales', Vol. V, 1917)

I quote from *Ancient Monuments in Wales and Monmouthshire 1917*: "The plan of the Church is unusual amongst the monastic churches of Wales. It consists of an aisleless nave, a transeptal chapel on either side of the nave and a long aisleless chancel". The pre-Reformation nave extended considerably further to the west and at some period, probably after the Dissolution, the nave was shortened. Unusual too amongst the monastic churches of Wales is the tower, finished off with a tall and well proportioned spire. It is located on the north side of the church, the base forming a porch, opposite which on the south side is situated the entrance porch. The decapitation of the nave stopped just short of the tower on the one side and the doorway on the other, the west end being finished off by a wall in which was inserted a late perpendicular window. The nave is of the unusual width of 33 feet. The chancel is plain and dignified. Several of the windows appear to belong to the latter part of the 13th century, they had become so ruined that Sir Gilbert Scott found a difficulty in their restoration. The transeptal chapels were doubtless built for tombs and chantry affairs. The churchwardens' report of 1720 states – "We present the two adjoyning to the church of Kidwelly, one werof belongs to the estate of Mudlescome, and the other to the estate of Llechdonney, to be out of repair, and ought to be repaired by the proprietors of the sayd estates, Arnold Hopkins, church-warden".

In the south transept (now the Lady Chapel) a tablet states that it was rebuilt in 1767, which must mean that it was then thoroughly repaired. In the chapel are a lady's monument and a civilian's monument, both believed to belong to the fourteenth century. Again I quote from *Ancient Monuments in Wales and Monmouthshire 1917*: "The tombs comprise one of great interest in memory of Lady Ysolda. This lady is without doubt the Lady Hawise who married Patrik de Chaworth and died in 1274. It is probably in her memory that the Priory Church was rebuilt". The lady's monument with her head carved in bold relief was dug up on the north side of the church on the 7th day of August 1846. There is also a slab bearing an incised cross of the fifteenth century, that has been appropriated by a comparatively modern alderman of the borough. Near the south-east angle of the inner wall is a good specimen of a well pre-served piscina.

The Virgin Crowned

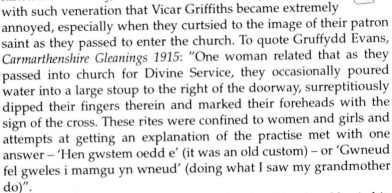

Within the church is a figure of the Virgin crowned (referred to earlier), holding the infant Saviour which is sculptured in pure white alabaster. Originally, it was full size and considered to be a fine example of fourteenth century art. At first it was installed in a niche situated behind the pulpit but later on it was transferred to an alcove located above the main entrance door. In the late nineteenth century, the women of Kidwelly regarded it with such veneration that Vicar Griffiths became extremely annoyed, especially when they curtsied to the image of their patron saint as they passed to enter the church. To quote Gruffydd Evans, *Carmarthenshire Gleanings 1915*: "One woman related that as they passed into church for Divine Service, they occasionally poured water into a large stoup to the right of the doorway, surreptitiously dipped their fingers therein and marked their foreheads with the sign of the cross. These rites were confined to women and girls and attempts at getting an explanation of the practise met with one answer – 'Hen gwstem oedd e' (it was an old custom) – or 'Gwneud fel gweles i mamgu yn wneud' (doing what I saw my grandmother do)".

Vicar Griffiths threw the figure into the churchyard and buried it, but there followed such an outcry from the townspeople that it was disinterred. However, those in authority, refused to return it to its original position so it was relegated to be left lying amongst the lumber in the church tower. When it was eventually rehoused inside the church, it was considerably damaged and renovation work was necessary. It is now displayed on a corbel on the east wall of the Sanctuary.

Hagioscope
The discovery of a squint, also known as a hagioscope, was a very exciting event which occurred during restoration activities in 1973. It is in actual fact a cavity formed at an oblique angle through the wall which exists between the vicar's vestry and the chancel, allowing one a view of the High Altar in the chancel. Exposure of the squint and the remains of a piscina (a stone basin built into the walls in which vessels used in the Communion Service were washed) led to speculation that this vestry was at some time a Chantry Chapel. This is contrary to a presumption in the only *History of Kidwelly* published in 1907, written by the vicar of the parish at that time – D. Daven Jones. However, there appears to be no reference to the hagioscope in any document or historical record of the church prior to its discovery. This is not too surprising as it had been concealed in the wall and well covered with thick plaster almost certainly since the 1530s. The earliest extant records date as far back as 1586, and so it was exposed to the light of day, in all probability for the first time in 400 years, when men working under the direction of a well-known craftsman, Mr Eddie Wilkins of Cross Hands, uncovered the channel in the chancel/vestry wall. The incumbent at the time was the Rev. Douglas L. Walters who stated and I quote – "The voluntary workmen were removing plaster on the chancel wall, in preparation for the re-pointing of the stonework underneath, when they discovered a completely different sort of dressed stone which initially appeared to be just like a picture frame. They cleared the rubble and found an angular cavity through the wall. It was very exciting, especially when we uncovered the other end of the squint in the vicar's vestry. It was quite thrilling to be able to see the altar from the vestry." It is thought that possibly the hagioscope was walled up at the time of the Dissolution of the Monasteries in the mid-1530s during the reign of Henry VIII. Subsequently, the medieval practice of using squints was discouraged. The hagioscope is structured about four feet above the floor and measures about three feet long and one foot wide. The design of a piscina close by almost

certainly confirms that the vestry was at one stage a chapel. Just slightly above the piscina and the squint and about six feet from the ground is located an entry onto a staircase and passageway.

There is no mention of a chapel in Daven Jones's chronicles, but he does surmise that the entry to the staircase – one of four built into the walls at various sites inside the church – was originally at first-floor level. He believed that the first-floor room above the vestry might have been an anchorite cell – the abode of a recluse. These cells (often attached to churches) were permanent homes for anchorites, who were either locked up or walled up at their own discretion, for a period of years or even a lifetime. The staircase leading from the vestry ends close to a superb wheel-shaped window, a circular loophole through which any occupant of the loft could see into the chancel. It may never be known for certain whether or not there was a chapel in the existing vestry, but the squint presents yet one more item of interest in our old thirteenth century church.

Fleur-De-Lis

In 1979 Canon Walters was associated with Mr Wilkins in yet another important discovery linking St Mary's with its medieval past. Above the entrance to the chancel vestry, stone memorial slabs of the nineteenth century, weighing a total of 17 cwts, had become unsafe and it was necessary to remove them. Subsequently, a large plaque bearing a decorative motif of the fleur-de-lis was revealed. Mr Wilkins said: "The slabs should never have been mounted there. Sections of the plaster work were damaged and renovation would entail a great deal of work". Canon Walters explained the significance of the ornamental art motif: "In medieval times the fleur-de-lis was accepted in France as the emblem of the Virgin Mary. It would usually be found on the northern wall of the church, as here at St Mary's. Its traditional link with the Arms of France and the Flemings cannot be questioned. At Kidwelly it is linked with the settlement of a Flemish community who in 1105 had to leave Flanders where parts of the low country in Belgium were flooded by the sea and therefore uninhabitable. Henry I, whose mother was a Flemish princess, allowed many of these unfortunate people to reside in this country, where a few settlements were established in Carmarthenshire, Pembrokeshire and the Gower. The immigrants lived under the protection of Norman castles, which would explain the reason for their presence in Kidwelly."

Interior of St Mary's Church, c.1930 – note the gas lamps
(*Photograph courtesy Author*)

Church Plate
The oldest existing vessel is a silver chalice which dates back to the reign of Queen Elizabeth I. It is elaborately embellished and bears the following Latin inscription – POCULUM ECLESIE DE KYD-WELLY 1574.

The chalice is one of the best specimens of Elizabethan ecclesiastical plate in the whole diocese of St David's.

Registers
The first register is dated 1626, and in this corner of Carmarthenshire is second only to St Ishmael (Ferryside) in antiquity. All the entries up to the year 1733 are recorded in Latin in a bold and legible calligraphy. Photostat copies only are kept in the Church.

Organ
The organ was brought from St Mary's Church in Swansea in 1907 and the purchase price was £281. The casing is inscribed with the words "Thomas Warne Fecit 1762". A successful fund-raising exercise in 1974 provided the money to restore the organ completely, giving it another lease of life.

The Font
The font is 'modern', taking the place of the one destroyed when the spire fell in 1884.

On the occasion of a visit by the Cambrian Archaeological Association to Carmarthen in 1875 there was exhibited a large model of the church made in 1842, which showed shutters on the windows, rendered necessary because of the fairs then held in the churchyard. My research yielded not a trace of the present whereabouts of this model.

A weathercock was installed at the top of the steeple in 1738 at a cost of five guineas. It was fashioned in copper and measured some six feet from point of beak to the end of the tail. In the year 1845 it was blown down in the wake of a storm. In the year 1740 a clock was attached to the church steeple at a cost of twenty pounds. In 1864 the existing clock was presented to the town by Owen Bowen Esq. of London, a pioneer of the Mynydd-y-Garreg Railway and Lime Works. When the tower was badly damaged by lightning in 1884 the interior workings of the clock were also badly damaged and it was 'on stop' for several years. However, in 1902 the clock was repaired and the dials raised to a higher elevation at the expense of the Borough in commemoration of the Coronation of King Edward VII.

The severely simple tower with its graceful spire may well be considered the most outstanding architectural feature of the whole structure. In fact the spire is of a design that is rarely seen in Carmarthenshire. It is certainly one of the most picturesque features in the district. The whole building is characterised by its simplicity and spaciousness. From the town square there is an excellent view of the impressive church building, standing back and slightly aloof from the mundane pressures of shopping chores and general street activity.

Memorial Tablets
The memorial tablets reflect extensively the history of Kidwelly through the ages, i.e.:

> The Kymers (Canal Builder) Thomas Kymer, Mary, Dorothy and Hester
>
> Johannis Brigstoke – Llechdwnny   –   1639
> Thomas Pardo, twice mayor of this town   –   1698

Owen Robert son of Mary, daughter of
William Brigstoke Llechdwnny   –   1721
John Howells, Carpenter of this town   –   1780

Anthony Jones, thrice mayor of this town
and the officer of customs in this port   –   1777

Margaret Price died 1757 – in her 35th year and
Ann Stephens died 1785 – in her 25th year
Wives of John Jenkins, Alderman of this town
7 of their children 3 by Margaret Price
4 by Ann Stephens all who died in infancy

George Roberts Alltcinadda   –   1783

Affixed on the inner west wall of the church are three appealing
memorials which were previously lodged outside.

John Howard   –   1722
Elizabeth Davenport   –   1733
Evan Davies, Clockmaker of this town   –   1835

the latter having a lathe and a grandfather clock displayed in the
Welsh Folk Museum, St Fagan's, Cardiff.

Two memorial tablets have been mounted on the south wall of
the nave to commemorate the men of the parish who gave their
lives in two world wars:

1. To the Glory of God and in memory of the fallen from this
   Parish.

                              1914-1919

Morgan Morgan	W. James	Oliver Evans
J. Tucker	Norman Williams	W. Lewis
D. Gower	George Roberts	A. Styles
D. J. Morgan	Sam Jones	Ernest Wild
Ivor Emanuel	W. J. Morgan	Sidney Jenkins
W. H. Davies	W. E. Davies	Tudor Jones
D. Hughes	Idris Evans	Frank Davies
W. Hughes	David Edmunds	F. Stephens
A. Hugh	A. Gilaspie	W. J. Anthony

Owen L. Edwards	S. Hughes	D. J. Howells
Wyndham Lewis	S. Sullivan	W. J. Lowe
F. Stokes	Oliver Jones	T. Miles
D. M. Davies	Mervyn Jones	J. Parry

Eternal Rest give unto them O Lord.

2. In Honoured Memory of the men in this Parish who gave their lives in the war.

1939-45

Reginald Anstee	Thomas King
John Collins	Arthur Lewis
Alec Gravell	Thomas Locke
Kenneth Hawkins	James Rogers
David A. Hudson	Trevor Rogers
Glyn John	Leslie Walters
Ivor Johns	E. William Thomas

Four stained glass windows add their own characteristic mark to the beauty of the building:

1. Located in the east wall of the sanctuary, presented by Sir Alfred Stephens in memory of his father and mother – Daniel and Catherine – in 1939.
2. Accommodated in the south wall of the sanctuary and donated in memory of Grace and Tudor Jones in 1993.
3. Erected in the south wall of the Lady Chapel in memory of John Richard and William Thomas Morgan.
4. Installed in the west wall of the nave in 1960, given in memory of Thomas Daniel Thomas, Glanmorfa.

Our former vicar, Rev. Canon Graham Davies, took me round the church pointing out many items of great interest. Canon Davies explained:

"Back in medieval times the Church was also a school and a theatre. In the nave was a rood loft and on this platform religious plays would have been performed, and in this way people learned more about the scriptures. You see, this ancient Church was a school, a theatre, as well as being a place of worship. When we go into Church today we have the habit of bowing to the cross, which really is an acknowledgement of God's presence."

He continued:

"Sometimes people come in here during the day, they want to get away from the hustle and bustle of the street; they just sit quietly taking in the atmosphere and the presence of God which emanates in the building. I feel that the very stones have been hallowed by centuries of prayer and worship, and I am very conscious of a divine presence."

The final word comes from Rev. Canon William Price, Vicar of the Parish:

"This outstandingly impressive and beautiful church is, of course, no museum. It is the spiritual home of a large and enthusiastic congregation, of all ages, which meets on Sundays for the Sung Eucharist and for Evensong. Prayers are also said in church throughout the week. The monks' Latin has been replaced by Welsh and English, but the liturgy of the Anglican Church in Wales has retained the essentials of the Benedictine tradition. Here too the age-old rites of baptism, marriage and burial continue, making the church deeply part of the life of the town.

We have a goodly heritage. Over the centuries the church has been restored and renovated; even during the eighteenth century, often regarded, wrongly, as period of neglect as far as churches were concerned, the Lady Chapel and Vestry were rebuilt, a new entrance door was provided, and a weathercock added to the spire. The present generation of parishioners is very aware of the need to preserve our inheritance, and to enhance its beauty. The church also has an important ministry to tourists and in this connection the church door is open from early morning until dusk every day to welcome visitors, who come from all over the world. Many townspeople too find it helpful to go into the church during the day to say their prayers and to find peace in its very special atmosphere.

The people of Kidwelly are very proud of their splendid church, a place of living worship, a place where prayer has been, and is, valid. Here is a place where we may still experience the beauty of holiness in traditional Anglican worship, and where the witness of past centuries mingles with the realities of the present and with our aspirations for the future."

Incumbents of the Parish

c.1111	Alwyn – the Priest of the town.	1808	Charles Phillips.
		1810	Charles Bowen.
1310	Thomas the Vicar.	1831	Richard Williams.
1399	Richard Watkyn.	1840	Thomas Griffiths.
1399	David Sandir.	1880	William Sinnett.
1442	Thomas Yororthe.	1888	D. Daven Jones, B.A.
1482	John David.	1908	Gruffydd Evans, B.D.
1490	John Gwynva.	1914	D. Ambrose Jones,
1491	John Cheyny.		M.A., Canon
1502	John Griffith.	1934	Evan J. Kingsbury,
1548	Edward Elmeley.		B.A.
1562	Giles Shires.	1958	Douglas L. Walters,
1597	Henry Fisher.		B.A., Canon
1626	Roger Pritchard.	1986	Graham J. Davies,
1669	David Evanson.		B.A., B.D. Canon
1701	Maurice Howell.	1997	D. T. William Price,
1734	William Jenkins.		M.A., F.S.A.,
1752	David Williams.		F.R.Hist.S., Canon

ST TEILO'S CHURCH, MYNYDD-Y-GARREG

The Church was opened in 1893 and celebrated its centenary with a series of special services and events. Records disclose that originally the property was purchased leasehold and in 1902 acquired the title of freehold. Burial services and marriage ceremonies cannot take place here because the building was dedicated, not consecrated. This house of prayer is an imposing presence occupying a quarter of an acre in neatly lawned grounds and favoured with outstanding views of the surrounding countryside. Constructed of hammer dressed local stone and roofed with Welsh slate, it accommodates a nave, sanctuary, a porch and vestry. Built by the firm R. Morgan & Sons, Builders, from plans prepared by W. Thomas, Surveyor, Kidwelly, the cost amounted to a sum in the region of £400.

Nestling snugly into the hillside, the church is sheltered by the towering heights of Mynydd-y-garreg. This is not a grand building with tablets and tapestries adorning its walls; here is a house of simplicity and beauty which over the century has witnessed true faith and loyalty. Even the very mention of the name St Teilo's Church (known to most by its familiar term 'Yr Eglwys Fach', the little church) is always acknowledged with fond affection. It stands in lonely silence within its unadorned grounds, always a welcome sight, sometimes unnoticed by passers-by but never forgotten by those who have visited it.

St Teilo Incumbents
1893 D. Daven Jones, B.A.
1908 Gruffydd Evans, B.D.
1914 D. Ambrose Jones, M.A., Canon
1934 Evan J. Kingsbury, B.A.
1958 Douglas L. Walters, B.A., Canon
1986 Graham J. Davies, B.A., B.D., Canon
1997 D. T. William Price, M.A., F.S.A., F.R.Hist.S., Canon

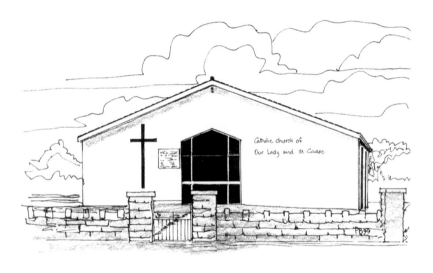

Catholic church of
Our Lady and St Cadoc

CATHOLIC CHURCH – OUR LADY AND ST CADOC

A small wooden building served as a church for the small congregation who attended the Catholic services since the time when World War II came to an end. The Church was dedicated to 'Christ the King' and a hand painted panel of 'the Christ' has survived from the early Church and is now a feature in the present building.

One Sunday in the early 1970s, the then parish priest, Father James Howard, announced at the end of Mass that it was time to start thinking about building a permanent Church. Father Howard, a very shrewd man, set up a small committee of nine people who were to report back with a plan of action. An architect was appointed – Colin Edwards of Llanelli – who drew up the plans for a church. Isaac Jones was engaged to erect the new building, with Eifion Lewis of Llanelli carrying out the necessary electrical work. The fine Crucifix located behind the altar was the work of Mr Thomas of the Carmarthen School of Art. Father Howard was overseer of the project and was most anxious that the building should not be too modern in style. His fears were allayed, as he was delighted when the Church was finally completed.

Subsequently, the question as to whom the new Church should be dedicated arose. A number of suggestions were put forward, and the Bishop had no hesitation in choosing Saint Cadog, as there was no other church in this diocese dedicated to him. A very ancient Church in Kidwelly was dedicated to St Cadoc, but today no trace of the church remains.

The new Church was opened on Sunday, 1 June 1975 when the building was consecrated by Bishop L. D. Fox. A large congregation attended the opening ceremony which included local priests and civic dignitaries. The Bishop placed a little phial of dust from the catacomb on the altar.

A plaque painted by Mr Eddie Murphy of Llanelli was placed in the Church to commemorate the consecration. Father Howard had requested that something in Latin should be inscribed on the tablet and the inscription declares:

Opened on June 1st 1975

by Rev. Langton D. Fox

Bishop of Meneva

LAUS DEO SEMPER

'Glory to God Always'

4

Nonconformist Chapels

BETHESDA CHAPEL (WELSH WESLEYAN)

A 'Wesleyan Brotherhood' was introduced in Kidwelly and thrived to such an extent that it became necessary for its members to consider building a chapel. It was built in 1816 on land granted by Earl Cawdor and the Municipal Corporation of Kidwelly under concurrent leases for a term of 999 years, at the annual rent of 2/6d. The chapel, a simple box-like structure, 'Bethesda' was constructed in about three months and was ready for worship on 9 June 1816. Members of the Borough Council contributed to the cost and also housed visitors who attended the opening services. The Welsh Wesleyan ministers present were John Davies, John Jones, Morgan Griffiths and Owen Rees, and members of the English circuit also shared the services. The collection amounted to almost £20. Bethesda was instrumental in greatly strengthening the Wesleyan cause in the town. Within 16 years the chapel was in need of renovation and the opportunity was taken to extend the meeting house; two new galleries were also added and the work was completed in seven months. Among the notable people present at the re-opening services on 9 December 1932 was an old stalwart of Methodism, James Buckley, who was at the time minister at Llanelli. Prior to the erection of an English

Bethesda Chapel, 1950s
(Photograph courtesy Author)

Wesleyan Chapel in 1866 both Welsh and English members held services in the chapel.

In 1916 Centenary Celebrations were held in the chapel. James Hansard, Acting Circuit Steward, and T. C. Hilliard, Superintendent of the Circuit, were present at the anniversary festival, and nearly all the nonconformist ministers in the town were present also – William Castellau Jenkins of Capel Sul, and D. Geler Owen and E. J. Herbert of the Calvinistic Methodists.

A local worshipper can recall that in the 1920s, a 'regular' at the Chapel by the name of Frank Rogers (known to all by his nickname Frankie Flwcs, due to his expertise at catching flwcs [a type of flatfish] down at the Town Quay) would bring out his mouth organ to accompany the hymn singing whenever the organist failed to turn up at services.

However, the Welsh cause had been declining for some years in spite of valiant attempts to keep it alive. It is now extinct and the last tangible link with early Wesleyan Methodism in Kidwelly vanished when the chapel was demolished in December 1962.

List of Ministers
No return.

HOREB CHAPEL, MYNYDD-Y-GARREG

Horeb Chapel, belonging to the Presbyterian Church of Wales, formerly known as the Calvinistic Methodists, was built in 1841 on land granted by the Municipal Corporation of Kidwelly, under a lease of 999 years at a nominal rent of one shilling a year. Rebuilt in 1863, it was enlarged again in 1877 when a gallery and interior fittings were installed. The old building stood until 1939 when a new and spacious chapel was opened on an adjoining site, the gift of the late Mr William Williams.

The first Sunday School was established on the hearth of Cwmsel, Nantygro, in 1832. The weekly meetings necessitated a more permanent building for the faithful, not the least being Thomas Job, later to become a minister at Cynwyl Elfed. Doctor Job, who studied in America for his degree, often claimed that he had brought the first load of building lime for the new Mynydd-y-Garreg chapel. He was to officiate there often during his successful ministry with the

Presbyterian Church. The vestry, also housing a basement flat for the chapel caretaker, was erected in 1900-01, and served for dozens of the village activities throughout the century. The church has produced innumerable characters, the late Rev. E. J. Herbert often citing Horeb as a church well capable of maintaining itself spiritually. Indeed, in days when prayer meetings for the first full week of the New Year were an essential feature of chapel life, Horeb could muster three or four volunteers each night and find that none had to participate twice.

The 'chapel on the hill' has produced three ministers for 'Yr Hen Gorff': John Beynon and Samuel Bryan Thomas, with the late Rev. George Davies also claiming to be closely connected with the village. Secretary of the Calvinistic Methodist Historical Society for years was the Rev. Tom Beynon, who delved long and deep into the historical traditions of his native heath, also his books are still on local bookshelves.

The chapel was renowned for one of the earliest Christmas services in Wales, the 5 a.m. Plygain attracting dozens of worshippers come rain, hail or snow. The new church of 1939 (with seating for 420) maintained the tradition, and only once, through illness, did the industrious Rev. Gwyn Davies Jones, throughout a 38-year ministry, fail to preside and deliver his seasonal greeting.

But Horeb would not have survived or flourished were it not for the faithful at Cwmsel: Dafydd Beynon, Richard Morris, Dafydd George, Thomas Morgan (senior), Thomas Beynon, John Prydderch, John Job, Ezekiel Williams, Elizabeth Morris, Thomas Beynon, John Howells, Thomas George, Thomas Morgan, Dafydd Evans, Jane Griffiths and Thomas Job. Thankfully, today's membership is similarly imbued with their exemplary vision and devotion. Part of the 150th anniversary celebrations were two successful television broadcasts from the *Dechrau Canu, Dechrau Canmol* series in 1992 maintaining Horeb's renowned musical traditions.

List of Ministers

Thomas R. Lloyd	1869
David Geler Owen	1872-1922 (buried at Horeb)
E. J. Herbert (Ieuan Wyn)	1923-1941 (buried at Cilycwm)
Gwyn Davies Jones	1943-1981 (buried at Drefach-Felindre)
D. Geraint Davies	from 1987

Today's deacons include Joel Gravell, ordained in 1964; Thomas Charles Beynon, Thomas Job Griffiths, William John Richards (1981) and Mrs Audrey Griffiths and Mrs Diana Pugh-Jones (1988).

MORFA WELSH PRESBYTERIAN CHAPEL/ WELSH CALVINISTIC METHODIST

The Methodist Revival developed in Wales during the 18th century as a result of the enthusiastic efforts of Howel Harris, William Williams (Pantycelyn), Daniel Rowlands (Llangeitho) and Peter Williams. Howel Harris included Kidwelly in his preaching tours on three or four occasions between 1740 and 1746 and stayed each time with the Pugh family of Morfa Bach Farm, some two miles to the east of the town.

During this period, Kidwelly was very much under the influence of wealthy families such as the Mansels of Muddlescwm (Middlescombe) and the Gwyns of Gwempa, who were loyal supporters of the Established Church. Representatives of the Methodist Movement were unlikely to be welcomed and during some of his earlier visits, Howel Harris encountered fierce opposition. It is said that Harris, on one occasion, began to preach in a street in the town but on being threatened by a group of local scoundrels, was forced to flee towards Mynydd-y-Garreg; he continued his sermon near the

site on which Horeb Chapel stands today. Peter Williams was also roughly treated during some of his visits to Kidwelly.

Nevertheless, these early Methodist Revivalists exerted considerable influence in the area, made many converts, and according to the Rev. Tom Beynon, a Methodist Society or 'Seiat' was established in Maesgwenllian as early as 1741. At this time, Mr William Bowen, farm manager at Llechdwnny Farm, was a prominent local leader of the Methodist Cause. The number of societies meeting in private houses increased and the need for a meeting-place was strongly felt. As a mark of respect to his farm manager, Mr Brigstocke of Llechdwnny, allowed the Methodists the use of an old barn at the eastern side of the town (now Priory Street) where they could meet, while retaining their membership of the Established Church. In 1782, Mr Brigstocke granted the worshippers a lease on the land and the building was converted into a Chapel, "Yr Hen Dŷ Cwrdd".

Welsh Methodism prospered in Kidwelly during the last years of the 18th century with Nonconformists from Mynydd-y-Garreg, Llansaint and Llandyfaelog making the journey, mainly on foot, to Kidwelly to worship in 'Yr Hen Dŷ Cwrdd'. Soon, the need for a larger building was evident.

The increase in Welsh Calvinistic Methodism at this time occurred against a background of economic affluence in the area. The Industrial Revolution was in full spate; the local tinworks employed many and the Quay was reaching the height of its prosperity with the export of coal and the import of all kinds of raw materials.

In response to the campaign by the Methodists for a larger Chapel, the Town Council granted them a 999-year lease on a piece of marshland on which to build.

With the help of voluntary labourers and sponsorship of such people as Mrs Stephens, Berthen, and Mrs and Miss Bevan, Pengay Farm, building work was soon commenced. The builder was a Mr Philip Luke of Carmarthen who was also a preacher with the Methodist Connexion. Stones for the building were transported from one of the Mynydd-y-Garreg quarries. The new Chapel was named Morfa (Sea-marsh) and was opened in 1830.

Soon after the opening of Morfa Chapel, Mr John Bevan, J.P., son of Pengay Farm, led a delegation of Chapel Elders to Llangadog, near Llandovery, to the Meeting of the Methodist Association ('Sasiwn') to invite them to meet at Kidwelly at the first available opportunity. As an incentive, he promised to pay all the Tollgate Charges for the delegates (the tollgate charges were at the time the cause of much discontent in rural Wales and, of course, featured as one of the main causes of the Rebecca Riots). The 'Sasiwn' accepted the invitation and eventually met in Kidwelly on a piece of land known as Parc yr Elflan in 1842. The Methodist Association Meetings were subsequently held in Kidwelly in 1859 on land known as Parc Shon Ditw, in 1888, 1921, 1944, 1959 and 1989.

During the late 1830s, the local Methodist Cause waned temporarily. This corresponded with a local economic depression and the opening of Horeb Chapel, Mynydd-y-Garreg in 1841 which resulted in the loss of many faithful and hardworking members.

However, during the second half of the 19th century, there was a resurgence in economic prosperity in Kidwelly. In 1858, Mr Jacob Chivers, an Englishman, bought the Tinworks which had previously been idle for some years, and installed new steam-driven machinery. Many local people found employment again, the standard of living improved and local businesses flourished once more. Chapel membership increased and included many tinworkers, farmworkers, craftsmen and shopkeepers – the last named reflected their prosperity with generous donations to the Chapel.

Sunday School
It appears from a report by The Royal Commission on Education that the Welsh Methodists had endeavoured to provide a Sunday

School in Kidwelly from an early date and, with the opening of the new Chapel and an increase in pupil numbers, it was felt that a separate schoolroom was needed for its activities and for other aspects of Chapel life. During the early 1880s it was decided to proceed with the building and the work was completed at a cost of £400; in 1886 the Vestry was officially opened. At this time J. G. Anthony (Alaw Gwendraeth), David Charles, Ebenezer Evans and Isaac Harries were elected Elders. Mr J. G. Anthony became a prominent businessman, a leading public figure in the town and a pillar of the Cause in Morfa Chapel as Elder and Precentor. In 1890, a branch Sunday School called Salem was opened in Priory Street to cater for the children of tinworkers living in the newly erected Gwendraeth Town, a street of 40 houses provided for tinplate workers and their families.

At the beginning of the 20th century, the Chapel was rebuilt and extended on the same site. It was reopened in all its splendour on 3 May 1908 and a graphic account of the occasion appeared in the *Llanelly Mercury* in the edition published on 7 May of that year.

Further renewals were completed with the installation of a pipe organ in 1923. The Manse was built and completed in 1951 on land donated by Mrs S. Davies, Orchard Villa.

List of Ministers

David Bowen	1832-1952
David Griffiths	1857
John Evans	1860
Thomas Lloyd	1869-1871
David Geler Owen	1871-1889
William Peregrine Jones	1889-1898
William Whitlocke Lewis	1906-1908
Caleb Williams	1909-1911
E. J. Herbert	1912-1942
Gwyn Davies Jones	1943-1981
D. Geraint Davies	1987

Elders and Trustees at the present time are Mr T. B. Gravell, Mr D. Arnold Gravell, Mr William Beynon, Mr Kenneth Palmer, Mr Gareth Gravell, Mr Hywel Gravell (Secretary), Mr David Gravell (Treasurer), Mrs Eunice Morgan (Organist).

The Rev. D. Geraint Davies adds his own personal comments in conclusion:

"It is with a feeling of pride that my ministry at Morfa Chapel Kidwelly and Horeb Chapel, Mynydd-y-Garreg which form part of a five chapel pastorate including Pembrey, Llansaint and Ferryside, follows such distinguished Ministers as the Rev. D. Geler Owen, E. J. Herbert and Gwyn Davies Jones, who between them gave over a century of services to the two Chapels.

Both Chapels were the result of visits to the area by the revivalist Howel Harris, as early as 1739, and to Peter Williams and others, who established Methodism in the locality, in the face of strong opposition from some of the leading citizens of the day. In the latter half of December 1740 a society was established at Maes Gwenllian which was the true basis of Methodism in the area. It was here that the great battle to defend the area against the spreading power of the Normans, that Princess Gwenllian was killed. So we have a rich history of spiritualism here for over two and a half centuries, with many of the farmhouses playing a prominent role in establishing a stronghold of Christianity, as did many of the nearby villages.

There is mention of Sunday Schools in the area as early as 1781, which gave rise to the Sunday School being set up at Cwmsel in 1832. So, when we think of the past and its rich local history, we feel that the present day inhabitants have lost a great deal of the religious fervour of the past, though the area continues to retain a faithful few, bearing witness to the mighty power of God, and who look forward to the new millennium with hope and faith, that the area will be blessed once more."

SOAR CHAPEL (INDEPENDENT)

Prior to the construction of a chapel in Mynydd-y-Garreg, worshippers had to tackle a long walk in order to attend services at Capel Sul in Kidwelly. Prayer meetings were held on Sunday afternoon at various houses in the village, and Mr and Mrs D. Gravel, Glandŵr, founded a Sunday School. As many of the older inhabitants were unable to make the long walk to Capel Sul, the need for a local chapel was very much in evidence.

A piece of land was leased from Mr William Jones, Penllwynteg,

for the sum of one shilling a year on a 99-year lease. Building the chapel commenced and the Minister of the mother chapel 'Capel Sul' wanted to name it Capel Gobaith. In the event the name chosen was Soar and the new chapel was opened on Sunday, 5 October 1869 by the Rev. Thomas Williams of Llanybri, W. E. Evans of Capel Seion, D. Evans, Nazareth and Dr Johns of Llanelli. The new Minister, the Rev. William Castellau Jenkins, was highly pleased with such a large attendance at the ceremony and by the wonderful collection of ten pounds and one shilling.

Whenever there was a need of any kind at Soar, Mr Oakley Harries of Garreg Farm was the person to turn to, as he was always very ready to help out. Names of the early chapel deacons are – T. Gravel, Parcymynydd, William Eynon, Blaenpant, William Jones, Penllwynteg, John Davies, Penhill, John Morgan, Highgate.

Special services were held on Sunday, 31 March, Tuesday, 2 April and Wednesday, 3 April, 1929, to celebrate the 60th Anniversary of the opening of the chapel. Ministers at the services were: Mr Edmund Gravel of Swansea, Rev. Emrys Jones of Pembrey, Rev. R. Jones of Sardis, and E. J. Herbert of Horeb. The Minister, Rev. E. Curig Davies, unveiled a plaque in the chapel erected in memory of Rev. William Castellau Jenkins.

List of Ministers

Rev. William Castellau Jenkins	1869
Rev. E. Curig Davies	1921
Rev. J. Aeronydd Enoch	1935

Rev. D. J. Rees	1942
Rev. D. Aeron Evans	1956-1968
Rev. Edgar J. Phillips	1969-1982
Rev. Haydn Davies	1984-1990

SILOAM CHAPEL (BAPTIST)

The Baptist persuasion in Kidwelly started circa 1796. An old brewery building in Alstred Street was acquired and a pulpit and benches were installed.

The Minister of Priory Street Chapel, Carmarthen, the Rev. Josiah Watkins frequently visited Kidwelly to preach at this chapel. His ministry was very successful, demonstrated by an increase in the number of worshippers The Rev. Watkins also started the Baptist cause in Llangyndeyrn and Ferryside around this time. When Ferryside was corporated, the Baptist members of Kidwelly united with them under the leadership of the same minister.

In 1797 dissenters gathered in the back kitchen of Mr Harries, Castle Farm, to attend meetings and prayer services. When the congregation increased Mr Harries kindly donated land which had previously been an orchard at the front of the farmhouse, to erect a chapel. The first Baptist Chapel in Kidwelly was completed and opened for prayers in 1821.

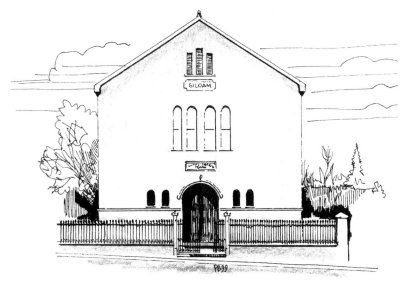

Over the years the congregation numbers grew rapidly and it was decided to build a larger chapel at the same location. A building fund was instituted in 1878, the members contributing weekly voluntary donations of one penny, three pennies or six pennies. The new chapel was opened in 1892 with seating for over 500 worshippers and the cost of building was £1500. It is believed that the first Minister was the Rev. Morris Morris. In 1830 a local boy, John Reynolds was ordained as Minister at Siloam and his ministry lasted for almost forty years.

In 1902 the Rev. H. R. Jones from North Wales became Minister at Siloam and the membership at that time was 104. The chapel was almost £1200 in debt and the new minister and members set about clearing this debt. By 1920 they had succeeded and special services of thanksgiving were held in September to mark the occasion. Special preacher at these services was the Rev. Ben Jones of Maesteg, a former member at Siloam. In 1928 a vestry was added to the main building with seating for about 200 people at a cost of £600. The chapel continued to flourish and by 1935 membership had increased to 200 worshippers.

In 1941 the Rev. W. O. Williams of Merthyr became the new Minister. He again was very faithful and successful and had the pleasure of seeing his only son Gareth become a minister. In 1966 a young minister, Rev. Meurig Thomas of Felingwm, Carmarthen, was ordained at Siloam. He left in 1973 after completing a very successful ministry. Since his departure the chapel has been without the services of a permanent minister. Services have been conducted by guest preachers. In addition to the Reynolds family, three more local persons were ordained into the Ministry from Siloam Chapel – Rev. Ben Jones, Maesteg, Rev. Richard Vaughan Jones, Aberbargoed and Rev. Glyn Williams, Aberdare.

On Sunday, 15 March 1992 special services were held to celebrate the chapel's centenary. The Rev. Meurig Thomas of Seion, Llanelli, conducted the services and Mr John Morgan gave a talk on 'Cyflwyno Hanes yr Achos'.

List of Ministers

Morris Morris			
John Reynolds	1830	Hugh Robert Jones	1902
George Reynolds	1860 } Joint	W. O. Williams	1941
John Reynolds	1861 }	Meurig Thomas	1966-1973

CAPEL SUL (INDEPENDENT)

The acquisition of land on which to build Capel Sul proved a difficult quest but in due time a piece of land in Ferry Road was leased from David Jones of nearby Pistyll Gwyn for a sum of one shilling per year on condition that he himself would be buried on the south side of the chapel, where he lies to this day. The old chapel was demolished but the cemetery remains.

The original chapel erected in 1787 was quite small but renovations and extensions were undertaken in 1873 and again renovations were carried out in 1905. In 1926 the chapel in Ferry Road was closed down and Rumsey House, a large imposing building in the town situated next to the bridge, was taken over. It was built in 1862 by T. W. A. Evans, Architect and later on a Mayor of Kidwelly. In 1920 Rumsey House was spotlighted when the notorious Harold Greenwood, then owner of the property, was tried and acquitted for the murder of his wife. Bought in 1923 by the independent congregation and converted to a chapel 1924-1926 by J. Harold Morgan of Carmarthen, the ground floor became the schoolroom and the two upper floors were combined as the chapel. A plaque retrieved from the 1831 chapel in Ferry Road is displayed in the ground floor lobby. The cost of converting Rumsey House into a chapel was somewhere in the region of £3000!

During the Second World War the vestry was put to good use as a canteen for ex-servicemen and women, and the chapel kitchen was used to house the labour exchange.

The chapel has been in existence for 200 years with nine ministers having held office:

David Davies	1787-1790
John Abel	1794-1819
David Griffiths	1820-1822
David Jones	1824-1867
William Castellau Jenkins	1867-1919
E. Curig Davies	1921-1933

William Aneurin Jenkins	1937-1957
Edgar James Phillips	1957-1982
Haydn Davies	1984-

Trustees are: Mrs Mair Morgan, Keith Gilasbey, Hywel Morgan, Myrddin Morgan and Lyn Jones.

TRINITY WESLEYAN CHAPEL
(TRINITY METHODIST CHURCH)

The Wesleyan Methodist Chapel was built in 1866 to meet the needs of the English members. Jacob Chivers, owner of the Tin Works, found the site – a cattle pound located near the town bridge, at one time occupied by William Raynor's shipbuilding yard. He agreed to move the cattle pound to another location and personally financed the deal. The building started as a small reading room, then became the schoolroom which was also used for divine services during the chapel's construction.

Both rooms were designed by T. W. Angell Evans, who freely gave of his professional services as an Architect of Kidwelly. Evans, a prominent Anglican, was also responsible for the provision of an ornamental tower and porch. When the building was completed

there was a seating capacity for 200 people and a gallery was provided for the choir. The estimated cost was £650.

The centenary of the demise of John Wesley occurred in 1891 and this event was commemorated by constructing an extension to the schoolroom at an estimated cost of £250.

The Centenary of the Chapel was celebrated in 1966 with a series of divine services during November and a Centenary Fund was set up for the maintenance of the Chapel.

List of Ministers

Joseph Higham	1866	J. Hetherington	
Nehemiah Smith	1867-8	Cleminson	1886-87
Jabez Chambers	1869-71	J. Arthur Aldington	1880-90
Joseph Shrimpton	1872-4	James Picot	1891-93
Samuel W. Beard	1875	William May	1894
John Turner	1876	Reuben R. Simons	1895-1896
Enoch Biscombe	1877-78	F. H. Hooper Labbett	1897-98
John Taylor	1878	A. Perry Gill	1899-1901
James Etchells	1879-1880	Clement A. West	1902
Edward Bowman	1881	William J. Hannam	1903-1904
Robert Pordige	1882	Thomas Roberts	1905-1907
George Gibson	1883-84	Sydney P. Jacoby	1908
James C. Brewer	1885	Thomas Roberts	1909-1911

Robert F. Atkinson	1912-1914	Ivor Trigg	1945-1947
William E. Thomas	1915-1917	Donald White	1948-1951
John B. Lee	1919-1921	Donald A. Davies	1952-1955
G. Rowland Owen	1922-1924	Maurice Cartledge	1956-1957
Harold A. Bishop	1925	George Lovell	1958-1961
James L. Smith	1926	Lewis J. Hayward	1962-1965
Reginald C. Stonham	1927-1928	Hedley Huxtable	1966-1970
Thomas Metcalf	1929	Harold Ridgeway	1971-1978
John R. Penistow	1930	Alfred Austin	1978-1981
William J. Roberts	1931-1934	Trevor Thomas	1981-1987
Goronwy Jones-Davies	1935	Fred Day	1987-1994
W. George Griffiths	1936-1940	June Mallabon	1994-1998
Donald A. Davies	1941-1944	Adelaide Wheeler-Cocks	1999-

In October 1998 a fire badly damaged the chapel building and completely destroyed the organ. By the kind permission of Canon William Price services were held at St Mary's Church while repairs were being carried out.

Present officials of the Chapel:

Secretary/Treasurer:	Mrs Margaret Morgan
Property Steward:	William Stanfield
Stewards:	Mrs Dorothy Jones, Mrs Carol Rees
Organist:	Miss Sian Rees
Communion Steward:	Mrs Mary Stanfield
Sunday School Leader:	Mrs Mavis Evans

THE APOSTOLIC CHURCH

The Apostolic Church began in Penygroes, South Wales in 1911, when a group of people with evangelistic and pentecostal beliefs started holding services in the village, first in the vestry of the Congregational Chapel, then in a butcher's shop, a salt store and later on, in the Council School. Today, the Apostolic Church is international with churches in sixty countries and an estimated membership of two million people. Remarkable progress when we consider this great work was commenced in the small village of Penygroes.

The Apostolic Church in Kidwelly began in 1919 when D. R. Thomas

and his family moved to Coleman Farm and held meetings in a large room in the farmhouse.

In 1934 the family moved from Kidwelly and Mrs Thomas's brother, Alexander Thomas, moved in to Coleman and continued the services on the farm. During the summer months, services were sometimes held outside and converts were baptized in a well located on the farm grounds.

By the 1940s the room used for meetings was too small to accommodate all who attended and a room was hired in the Pelican Hotel (now the Council Offices) the room used being the former Labour Exchange.

Soon this room too was outgrown and the congregation held their meetings in the Welsh Wesleyan Chapel, Bethesda, which stood in the shadow of the castle and was known as the 'Wesle Fach', now sadly no longer in existence. The Chapel continued being used by members of the Welsh Wesleyan congregation but was shared by the Apostolic Church, services being held at different times.

Eventually, it was decided that the Apostolic congregation needed to purchase a building of their own and in 1956 the church in Gwendraeth Town (previously owned by Capel Sul and used as a Sunday School room) was purchased. Services were held there until 1991, when the building was declared unsafe for public use because of subsidence, a large crack having appeared in one of the walls. The church was therefore demolished and a new building erected on the same spot, the new building being opened in November 1991.

5.

Industries

THE CLOTH TRADE

Carding, spinning and cloth weaving were some of the prevalent skills of the early Welsh. From local supplies of wool the native hand looms wrought a rough type of cloth, or blanket called 'brychan'. After the introduction by the Flemings of the fulling mill in the 14th century, Welsh cloth was manufactured on a substantial scale. There seems little doubt that by this time cloth making was an eminent industry in Kidwelly. The Flemish settlers are accredited with having introduced the manufacture of worsted and woollen fabrics as well as the art of dyeing. Whilst the Normans and the English were the guardians of the district, it is very probable that in the community the business of cloth making was undertaken by the Flemish, a skill for which they had the greatest aptitude. The accounts of the Duchy of Lancaster in the year 1369-1370 mention two fulling mills – 'the farm of the fulling mill' and 'the fulling mill called Bordculle'.

A large woollen export trade developed between Wales and England. In the 15th century, the cloth trade flourished considerably, so that Welsh cloth was found not only in the fairs and markets of Wales but also in the towns of the border counties, as well as the great cloth fair at St Bartholomew in London.

FARMING

Gerald of Wales (Giraldus Cambrensis) writing in 1188 on his famous journey through Wales, states that: "the Welsh were at that time for the most part a pastoral people who lived in scattered homesteads and not in towns or villages". For most folk, means of sustenance was derived from their animals, with oats, milk, cheese and butter. Oats, barley wheat and vegetables were grown in only small quantities.

The Norman occupation led to new conceptions in farming with emphasis on arable cultivation. A Norman lord would in the first instance secure himself and his followers by constructing a castle, then adjacent land would be farmed using a manorial system. This was based on arable cultivation in large open fields, divided  into several strips. Crops such as oats, barley, wheat and greenstuffs for fodder were grown in rotation. Each field would remain untilled every third year so as not to exhaust its fertility. In these manorial settlements, with their ploughed and sown strips cultivated in common by the peasants, the rearing of animals was regarded as being much less important than growing food crops.

The Welsh carried on their customary method of pasturing cattle, goats, sheep and swine alongside the manorial system. The inhabitants paid to the Norman lord the dues which were previously paid to their prince or chieftain and payment was made in kind, e.g. cattle, by which means the main wealth of the tribesmen had been measured for centuries. Gradually, cash transactions were substituted for animals.

In the Middle Ages there were three corn grist mills set on the Gwendraeth Fach river. They were Castle Mill in the vicinity of the town bridge, Middle Mill and Upper Mill also known as Cadoc's Mill by reason of its proximity to a Celtic Church dedicated to St Cadoc (all traces of this church have vanished).

In the 14th century the lordship of Kidwelly was part of the vast possessions of the House of Lancaster for which the mills provided an important source of profit. The tenants of the lordship were obliged to bring their corn harvests to be ground at the mills, to assist in hauling heavy material, and to pay a toll to the miller. A service was also demanded whereby every freeholder was liable to find a man to scour and cleanse the mill ponds on one day in May each year.

Prior to the Industrial Revolution, farming was by far the largest employer of labour in the district.

SHIPPING AND SHIPBUILDING

In bygone days Kidwelly was an
ancient port and there are records
that testify its importance as a sea-
faring town:

> "In 1229 permission to trade
> with Gascony was given by
> patent of Henry III to Robertus
> de Cadewely, magister navis"
> (Robert of Kidwelly ships mas-
> ter).
> Pat Rolls Henry III. 1229

"Safe conduct until Michaelmas for Eudo-la-Zushe conveying
by water, corn and other victuals by his own sailors from
Bridgwater, Totnes, and Dartmouth to Pembroke, Kaermer-
dyn, Kedwelly and Sweyneseye, for the support of those persons who are there on the king's expedition against Llewellyn
and his accomplices in rebellion!"

Pat Rolls 5, Edward I. Feb. 1277

At times of war in foreign parts ships from Kidwelly and other
local ports were frequently taken over by the king, to convey troops
to the Continent. By the mid-13th century the town emerged as an
important trading port linked with Ireland and the ancient French
ports of Gascony and Aquitane. The main cargoes comprised commodities such as corn and general provisions for the garrison.

After the turbulence of the earlier centuries, the town expanded
in the more peaceful and settled conditions of the 14th century, its
commercial prosperity being brought about by immigrant families
and overseas links. The Port of Kidwelly was named in a writ in
1331 issued by Edward III, for William Wrench appointed by
Arnold Micol, King's Sergeant, to act as his deputy in the office of
Chief Butler in the port. Despite a lack of documentary evidence it
is said that several small quays on the tidal reaches of the Gwendraeth Fach made Kidwelly the busiest trading port in South Wales,
and was doubtless the landing place for pilgrims from Devon, Cornwall, Brittany and other parts of the Continent. A prominent burgess

family, namely the Aylwards, were actively encouraged in the shipping of wool by Henry, Earl of Lancaster, Lord of Kidwelly, who in 1341 invested two of them, Walter and Adam, with £100 each, to be returned with profit at the end of the year. Another member of the family, Thomas, was in the year 1357 exporting hides to Gascony. A notable merchant was John ap Owen who in the 1390s became one of the leading exporters of wool in south-west Wales. In the 'John of Kidwelly', a typical merchant vessel, broad beamed, rounded bow and stern and single mast, he shipped as many as 50 sacks of wool to London annually. Commodities brought in by sea to South Wales ports consisted of red and white wines, salt, salted fish, fresh and dried fruits, sugar, spices, oil and tar. Exports were mainly of wool, woollen goods, hides and leather.

Steady growth of both town and port was maintained throughout the 15th century. By the early years of the 16th century, however, these trading links were faltering.

The town which had been Carmarthen's strong rival as a port in the medieval period suffered a severe setback when the Gwendraeth estuary became silted up with sand and mud. The trade of the town – almost entirely seaborne – began to decline as passage to the quays became possible for only the smallest vessels, and the port gradually lost its shipping trade. The English traveller – Leyland – in the 1540s described the borough as 'sore and decayed'. At that time the town contained 100 houses, and though its seaborne commerce had ceased, it continued to hold the special trading privileges granted by its charter. Camden, in his 'Britannia in 1586' observed:

"The harbour is stated to have been almost choked up with sandbanks. The sandbanks at the mouth of the Gwendraeth River had shifted and almost blocked up the channel, preventing entry by larger vessels which conveyed goods from Bristol and further afield."

The 17th century was a period of stagnation and isolation for the town, yet it was one of the first in Wales during the following century to receive the benefits of the Industrial Revolution. Industries sprang up one after another, the results of which led to a revival of the local shipping industry. The mouth of the Gwendraeth was dredged, quays were built and a canal was created – the first in Wales. The port flourished again, the shipping trade resumed and the town was reborn. There were in existence at least three quays

Kidwelly Docks, early 1900s
(Photograph courtesy Author)

where ships were laden and unladen – of these only one remains.
Of the other two – Kymer's Quay which was adjacent to the 15th
century bridge that spans the Gwendraeth Fach and Coney Quay
on the right bank of the Gwendraeth Fawr above Commissioner's
Bridge which was built at a later date (1842) – there is little trace.
Coal was conveyed to London, Bristol and the West Country by sea.
There was a good passage linking Kymer's Canal to the quay and
twenty or more ships often queued in the river waiting to be loaded
with coal. Proof of the revived interest in the town is the astonish-
ing number of mariners from Devon and the West Country in the
Burgess Roll. These men paid enrolment fees up to thirty times
higher than those paid by residents of the borough for the same
privileges. Between the years 1728 and 1793 no fewer than 61 names
of mariners from England (chiefly the West Country) were added to
the Roll.

Kidwelly, as did many Welsh ports in the 18th century, had its
own shipbuilding yard, situated on the site now occupied by the
English Wesleyan Chapel. The most successful local shipbuilder
was William Raynor, who had earlier been engaged in building and
repairing barges for Kymer's Canal. In 1803 he leased a portion of
the river bank close to the town bridge for a building yard. From

here he launched a variety of vessels – brigs, snows, sloops – the largest being the brig 'Margaret' of 163 tons and built in 1814. Parish registers confirm that Kidwelly was a busy mercantile centre, since in addition to mariners, pilots, captains, records show an abundance of craftsmen dependant on the sea, e.g. shipwrights, ship's carpenters, ropemakers and anchorsmiths. Further confirmation of its nautical character is supplied by the names given to inns and public houses – The Pilot Boat, The Jolly Sailor, The Hope and Anchor, The Ship and Castle and the Yarmouth Arms.

Many of the local industrialists owned a small fleet, such as Messrs. Haselwood & Hathaway, proprietors of the tin works. In 1801 the partners owned the 'Elizabeth and Mary of Kidwelly', a sloop of 35 tons; the 'Mary of Kidwelly' a brigantine of 53 tons; and the 'Bold Harry', a sloop of 21 tons built at Kidwelly. They also owned shares in the 'Eleanor' built by William Raynor.

The following quotes from local newspapers *Carmarthen Journal* and *Llanelly Guardian* highlight the town's maritime importance.

1805.　On Friday last was launched from the yard of William Raynor, shipbuilder at Kidwelly, a beautiful brigantine called the 'Eleanor', David James commander, burden 150 tons. She went off in the most majestic manner, amidst the applause of a great number of spectators.

1806.　The 'Kidwelly Castle' of Kidwelly, Captain Davis of 4 guns and 10 men was captured on her voyage from Lisbon to Bristol, by the San Pedro. The Spanish privateer of 7 guns and 52 men won after an action of nearly two hours.

1813.　On Monday last, the master of a vessel was fined £5 for discharging his ballast within a high water map in the borough of Kidwelly. The information was reported by Walter Thomas one of the pilots of the port.

1813.　The rapid and progressive restoration of the ancient harbour of Kidwelly is well under way, enabling ships of small burden to pass to and from the river into the channel, thus promising a ready facility for vessels to navigate to the port, and carry away by sea the extensive mineral products of the district.

1813.　On Friday, a young man was unfortunately killed at Kidwelly during the launching of a ship the 'Agenoria', a snow, of 105 tons. The accident occurred by the bursting of an old swivel fired on the occasion of the launch.

1814.   A fine new brig, the 'Margaret' built by William Raynor of
        Kidwelly, sailed from Bertwn Quay laden with 260 tons of
        coal for the London market.
1814.   The sloop 'Friends Good Will' of Laugharne on passage
        from Kidwelly to Laugharne, fully laden, sank off St Ishmael's
        Church.
1816.   The 'William of Plymouth' from Newfoundland, loaded with
        sealskins and oil, was grounded on Cefn Sidan sands near
        Kidwelly in a heavy gale.
1818.   Two men were committed to Carmarthen County goal,
        charged with breaking into a cellar at Kidwelly and stealing
        a quantity of wine and port the cargo of the Spanish Brig
        'Bergettor', lately stranded on sandbanks near the town.

During the first decade of the 19th century the movement of sand
was as in previous years, causing problems for navigation. A new
channel was excavated but this exercise solved the difficulty for but
a short space of time. The Kidwelly & Llanelli Canal Company,
formed in 1812 made further fruitless efforts to clear the shifting
sands. The Company had been set up to cater for the expanding
coal production in the district, in conjunction with an improved and
extended canal system to serve the Gwendraeth Valley. In 1820 John
Rennie, the engineer, was called in by the directors. His report was
not encouraging and the costs of improving the approach to the
dock were far too high. In 1840 the canal system was linked to the
new Burry Port Harbour, where the water was deeper and more
appropriate for shipping purposes. Consequently, the bulk of the
coal traffic was diverted from Kidwelly. It was not the end for
Kymer's Dock, however – it continued to be in use up to the early
years of this century mainly for shipments of coal to Laugharne,
Carmarthen, St Clears and Llanstephan. In the 1890s and early 1900s
the nearby Stephens Silica Brick Works used it extensively. The
steamship 'William Dawson' in 1894 loaded 320 tons of bricks for
Middlesborough, the 'Lynx' 250 tons for Cumberland and the 'Captain Cook' and the 'Dunvegan' with similar amounts for Glasgow
and Newport respectively. By 1914 this trade was undertaken by
rail and the last faithful operators to tie up under the coal chute
were crews of boats from Llanstephan in the 1920s. Thereafter it fell
into complete disuse.

   After centuries of maritime activity, which undoubtedly contributed to its growth and prosperity, Kidwelly finally turned its back

on the sea. Today's inhabitants of the town and visitors alike, standing on the bridge and looking down river, must be forgiven for not realising this this was a port of consequence, so utterly have all traces of the former activity vanished, as though it had never been.

Smugglers

"The port of Kidwelly which served Carmarthen town was also at one time a centre of both smuggling and piracy. During the reign of Elizabeth I, pirates exercised their illicit operations from Kidwelly and there was good reason to suppose they were aided and abetted by some of the tradespeople of the town.

The squire 'class' of South Wales demanded a large number of luxuries in their homes; these were generally very heavily taxed and were also extremely scarce. When luxury goods were bought by merchant shippers abroad they were usually sent to the larger centres of population, such as London and Liverpool and excluded the poor towns such as Carmarthen situated in the backwoods of Wales. It is here the smugglers really came into their own – the pirate stole the goods, the smuggler ensured they eluded the excise men and in this way the contraband found its way into the homes of the gentry.

A SHIP HAS BEEN SIGHTED in this quarter ENGAGING IN THE UNLAWFUL ACT OF

SMUGGLING

whosoever can lay information leading to the capture of this ship or its crew *will receive a reward of*

£500

From His Majesty's Government

This 19th day of October 1782

Smuggling poster
(Photograph: 'Welsh Smugglers',
K. C. Watkins, 1975.)

We can rest assured that both pirate and smuggler were well paid for their trouble. Goods such as ginger, spices, brass ornaments, perfumed soaps, pewter, pins, buttons, vinegar, sugar, tropical fruit, wines and other liquors – the list is endless."

from *Welsh Smugglers*, K. C. Watkins, 1975.

Ships Built at Kidwelly, 1787 to 1823

1787   ALBION. Brigantine. 71 tons.

1788   KIDWELLY CASTLE. Sloop. 35 tons.

1789   ELIZA. Sloop. 32 tons.

1798   JOHN AND SALLY .Sloop. 31 tons. Built by William Raynor.

1799 BEDFORD. Barge. 40 tons. Built by William Raynor.
1801 PRINCESS ROYAL. Brigantine. 177 tons.
1803 MARY. Sloop. 47 tons.
1803 COMMOTE. Brigantine. 89 tons.
1803 KIDWELLY CASTLE. Snow. 118 tons. Captured and sunk by
       a Privateer in 1805.
1803 EXPEDITION. Sloop. 51 tons.
1804 BOLD HARRY. Sloop. 22 tons.
1804 ELEANOR. Snow. 114 tons. Built by William Raynor.
1805 COURIER. Sloop. 28 tons. Built by William Raynor.
1805 ENTERPRISE. Sloop. 43 tons.
1806 ROYAL RECOVERY. Brigantine. 80 tons. Built by William
       Raynor.
1810 MERLIN. Sloop. 42 tons. Built by William Raynor.
1813 AGENORIA. Snow. 105 tons. Built by William Raynor.
1814 MARGARET. Brigantine. 163 tons. Built by William Raynor.
1816 ELIZABETH AND ANN. Sloop. 49 tons.
1819 PERCYS. Smack. 35 tons. Built at Dan y Lan (St. Ishmaels) by
       Philip Thomas, Kidwelly.
1823 GEORGE AND JANE. Schooner. 57 tons.

THE LIME INDUSTRY

The earliest reference to lime kilns in the area is from a Kidwelly
Corporation Minute Book dated 20th November 1682 when an
order was made – "granting a lease to William Dyer, Alderman, the
liberty to erect lime kilns in the vicinity of Mynydd-y-Garreg".
Subsequent Corporation minutes bear record to kilns in 1785: "That
a lease be granted to Walter Mansel and Edward King of a certain
part of Mynydd-y-Garreg for erecting a lime kiln for a yearly rent of
one shilling". Another reference is found on May 31st 1790: 'A lease
is granted to Herbert Lloyd, his heirs and assigns, for a term of
three lives, of a portion of Mynydd-y-Garreg whereon to erect a
Lime Kiln". At later dates, far more extensive lime kilns were constructed by Mr Owen Bowen, Mr Edward Threlfall and Mr Alexander
Young.
    In 1861 Kidwelly Corporation agreed to allow Mr Owen Bowen
the right to work limestone, and for a few years at least he operated
his own lime kilns.

Maes Gwenllian, Mynydd-y-Garreg – showing Threlfall's lime kilns in the background, c.1930s

(Photograph courtesy Author)

Edward Threlfall, at one time owner of the Gwendraeth Valley Railway – Kidwelly to Mynydd-y-Garreg – established a very impressive block of seven lime kilns in Mynydd-y-Garreg in 1872. I quote from the *Llanelly Guardian*, 11th April 1872:

> "Kidwelly and Mynydd-y-garreg line has been purchased by Mr Threlfall and is now a fair way to completion. On Saturday a ceremony of laying the foundations of new lime kilns in connection with the railway was performed after an agreeable introductory speech by Mr Jacob Chivers, Velindre, and by Miss Threlfall and was witnessed by a large concourse of people. A cold collation was partaken of by over 200 persons including employees. The weather was exceedingly favourable, Alderman Thomas addressed the assemblage. The bells from the tower of old St Mary's rang many peals at intervals in honour of the day's festivities."

In 1876 Alexander Young opened up a stone quarry and then built five lime kilns in an impressive block alongside the lane from Penymynydd Farm to Graig Farm. Young, the owner of the local brickworks, built these kilns adjacent to the railway line in Mynydd-y-Garreg.

Lime had been used for agricultural purposes for very many years

T. B. Gravell on the footplate. Thomas John Evans securing the load with the
original lorry used to haul stone and lime from Mynydd-y-Garreg.
The occasion: taking a party camping to Tenby, 1933.

(Photograph courtesy Peter Evans)

The kilns on the hillside in the distance are thought to be those built by Owen Bowen,
c.1863. The larger kilns in the foreground were built by Edward Threlfall in 1872.

(Photograph courtesy M. R. C. Price)

but now a new market opened up with an industrial demand for the product. Early maps of the area show many small lime kilns scattered around the district. These were in the main owned by local farmers producing lime for their own use. Many accidents occurred and I quote from the *Llanelly Guardian*, June 1832:

> 'A dreadful accident occurred when a farm servant was found dead under a lime kiln near Kidwelly. It is presumed that the deceased, having partly loaded his cart with lime, went under the shafts so as to throw up the remainder. The verdict of the Coroner's Jury was 'accidental death'."

Local industrialists constructed three impressive blocks of lime kilns in the district, but older residents of the locality can recall only one in operation which was located near Newtown, Mynydd-y-Garreg. They all recall that these kilns were a work of art, huge blocks of dressed stone that should never have been dismantled – today they would have been a tourist attraction. Several residents were pleased to recall incidents from the past. Local farmer Mr Desmond Jones remembers going to these kilns near Newtown with a horse and cart, returning with a load of lime to be used to white-wash the farmhouse and outbuildings and to spread on the fields. The method used to heat up local limestone resulted in an end product, lime of the highest quality.

Mrs Annie Mary Owen who lived in the row of cottages at Newtown, near to the lime kilns, recollects that during the war local people would regularly shelter in the kilns during air raids. On one occasion, a bomb landed half a mile away, near to Rogerley Farm, which on impact shook the whole area, including the kilns. When the people eventually emerged from the kilns there was laughter all around, as they all looked like ghosts – covered from head to foot with white lime.

The late Thomas John Evans recounted a tale of two workmen arriving at the kilns one morning to be greeted with a shout for help. They were unable to trace where the cries came from, until on looking down into an empty kiln adjacent to the ones in production, they discovered that a man had fallen into the kiln. It seems he was returning from courting a lady friend in Mynydd-y-Garreg, had taken a short cut, got lost in the darkness and fallen into the kiln. He had spent the whole night there and when the workmen rescued him, he had suffered only a few cuts and bruises from his ordeal.

Mr Evans also recollected that lorries collected limestone from the Meinciau Quarries to be delivered to the lime kilns. Sometimes when reversing the lorry to tip the load into the kiln, the vehicle would be manoeuvred too far causing the brick work at the edge of the kiln to crumble and collapse. This resulted in the rear wheels of the vehicle sliding over the edge of the kiln and becoming immobile. Many a time was he involved in the very difficult and dangerous job of releasing the vehicle, and apart from the danger of a nasty drop, heat rising from the kiln was also proving to be a hazard.

Local businessman T. B. Gravell, made use of road transport to haul the lime and signed a contract with Rock Products Ltd. He made considerable use of the kilns; when his business was at its peak each of the seven lime kilns could be producing as much as 27 tons of lime a day, and road transport was the means of deliveries. Mr Gravell's activities in Mynydd-y-Garreg ceased in the 1960s.

Alexander Young's impressive lime kilns remain standing, whereas the site of Threlfall's huge lime kilns is now but a steep overgrown bank.

COAL INDUSTRY

Thomas Kymer started mining for coal around the middle of the 18th century, at his Great Forest Colliery, located outside Kidwelly at Carway. This is the only reference to coal in the period 1700-1800, and is probably one of the oldest anthracite collieries in Carmarthenshire. Although Leyland, around 1536, describes 'digging coles elles scant in Kidwellye land', Kymer, a Mayor of the Borough, was the first capitalist to exploit the mineral wealth of the Gwendraeth Valley. Despite a lack of documentary evidence of coal mining during this period, nevertheless there is at Carmarthen Record Office a wages list dated 1765, which is proof of the colliery's existence at that time.

30th March 1765
Labourers Pay List for Great Forest Colliery:
Payment on behalf of Thomas Kymer made by William Gwyther for work performed by labourers in raising coal and culm, felling timber for the colliery, loading barges, drawing carts, hedging, ditching and packing coal. There were 19 employees listed. I quote a few examples:

	days	at p.d	£. s. d	Signed or mark
John Morris	25	10	1.0.10	
Thos Gravel	24	8	16.0	
Walter Richard	24	6	12.0	
Martha Morris	21	4	7.0	
John Treharne	12½	8	8.4	

Minutes of the Corporation refer to coal storage at earlier dates:

1737. Lease of coal yard from John Collins to Walter Rees. Burgages consisting of old walls and waste ground since walled in and converted into a coal yard near the town bridge. – Hall day.

1738. Anthony Rogers and Charles Gwynn have the liberty of building and erecting a coal house on the bank on town lands near a certain place called Rhyd Morris Cross, 20 to 30 foot square. Rent 20s year – Hall day.

The colliery produced appreciable amounts of coal in the last two decades of the 18th century which was used mainly for domestic purposes and lime burning. Kymer built a canal to convey the output from his coalpits and limestone quarries to Kidwelly Quay. Coal was transported to Carmarthen, Llanstephan, Laugharne, Ferryside, Cardigan and St Clears. Coal was also shipped further afield to London, Bideford and the Channel Isles. The inventory of the Carmarthen Tinworks showed that coal was imported from Kidwelly in 1800, in barrels, in three small sloops. I quote from Black's *Guide to North and South Wales* dated 1851: "The inhabitants of Kidwelly are employed working coal, smelting iron and making tinplate, weekly market, population 1563."

KYMER'S CANAL

Earlier traders had used rivers and seaways frequently on account of the wretchedness of the roads. Thomas Kymer transported coal by river for some years but delays were encountered because the river sometimes changed course and was navigable only on spring tides. Kymer developed what was 'the first authentic canal in Wales', to facilitate the transport of coal from his coalpits situated higher up the valley down to the sea.

The bridge at Pwllyllygod, 1950s
(Photograph: W. H. Morris Collection)

Built between 1766 and 1768 the canal conveyed anthracite and culm from the coalpits and limestone quarries at Pwllyllygod and Great Forest to ships on the Gwendraeth Fach river below Kidwelly. Three miles long and twenty-six feet wide, excluding the towing paths and bulwarks, the canal was furnished with two passing places, one at Muddlescwm and one at Morfa; there was also a turning bay near the wharf at Pwllyllygod. Locks were not necessary. Several bridges which were built across the canal have either disappeared or have been altered, but at Pwllyllygod there remains a secluded bridge, superbly arched, which conveyed a tramroad from the pits, bringing the coal across the Gwendraeth Fach to the waiting barges.

Yet within a century of Kymer's assay into capitalism, the era of the canal was over in this part of the world. In 1865 the Canal Company became a Railway Company, and a track was laid up the valley alongside and in many places over the bed of the old canal.

IRON WORKS

Kidwelly Ironwords seem to have commenced towards the end of the 17th century and were owned by Henry Owen in 1720. Between

Falls of the Old Forge, Kidwelly, c.1900
(Photograph courtesy Author)

the years 1720 and 1748 bar iron was being produced in small quantities. The forge was situated on the banks of the Gwendraeth Fach River, about a mile north-east of the old borough of Kidwelly. Situated 100 feet above sea level it had an old mill race (one of the features of these early forges) connected to the Gwendraeth River. The area is well supplied with water, as is demonstrated by the presence of springs in the region, and this was one of the important factors in the location of the forge. Other factors prevailing were the presence of local supplies of iron-ore at Mynydd-y-Garreg and the location of the forge to the bridging point of the river.

TINPLATE MANUFACTURE

This section draws heavily on *Kidwelly Tin Plate Works – A History,* W. H. Morris. The tinplate industry was established in Kidwelly in 1737, making it the second earliest works in Britain after Pontypool. I quote from the Order Book of Kidwelly Corporation – "On August 14th 1737, Charles Gwyn of Kidwelly, tinman, was given the liberty of erecting on town lands called Bank Broadford, a rolling mill and 'other conveniences for a Tin Work'." Bank Broadford lay about a mile north of the town on the bank of the Gwendraeth Fach River. Later that year he was granted a lease enabling him to build a rolling mill and to make a weir to dam and pond up the water for the use of the said mill and works. Bank Broadford was an ancient and well established crossing point of the river and Gwynn was, therefore, required to build a bridge across his water courses to allow travellers to pass and re-pass. Kidwelly, a port since the Middle Ages, was well placed for the import of tin from Cornwall and for the export of the finished product. South and West Wales produced the 'tough iron' malleable and strong, most suitable for the production of tin plate.

In subsequent years several owners found great difficulty in raising sufficient capital to finance the works. It was purchased in 1780 by Leonard Bilson Gwynn for the sum of £1370. By 1801 it had changed hands again, the new owners being Benjamin Haselwood and Henry Hathaway who carried out necessary repairs and re-building. On completion they erected a plaque inscribed with their names and the claim that the works were the oldest in the kingdom. Little information has survived to illustrate operations under the partnership. By 1806 the works was again in serious financial straits.

In 1838, the bells of Kidwelly were rung to celebrate the takeover of the works by Herbert Dowman, but for the next 20 years, there was little cause for rejoicing. Dowman, and later, his brother Henry,

Kidwelly Tinplate Works, c.1930
(Photograph courtesy Author)

Tinplate workers, 1920s
(Photograph courtesy M. R. C. Price)

lacked resources and had little knowledge and experience of the industry. Despite a rail line running through Mynydd-y-Garreg very near to the Tin Plate Works, no attempt was made to link up during the broad gauge era, not even early on in the standard gauge period – surely an expression of doubt about the commercial worth of the tin plate works at that time. In 1858, Jacob Chivers purchased the works for the sum of £2,225. Up to this time, the machinery had been propelled by water power. Jacob Chivers was joined by Thomas Bright as a working partner and they installed the first steam engine at the Kidwelly works. By 1874, the firm now known as Messrs. Chivers & Son, had three mills in operation – two operated by steam, the other by water – a forge and a tin house. As late as 1880, a siding was laid into the works which linked up to the Gwendraeth Valleys Company's short mineral line connecting to the Great Western Railway main line at Kidwelly. From here, tinplate was sent to the ports of Llanelli or Burry Port and shipped to Liverpool for trans-shipment to America, the main export market for the British Tinplate Industry.

In 1879, Jacob Chivers handed over the works to his son, Thomas Chivers, who began a large scale expansion. He installed six additional mills powered by two large Fowden steam engines and by 1882, nine mills were in operation. As a result of this expansion, there was a marked increase in the work force and dramatic increase in the population of town and parish. What is significant too is that by 1881, for the first time, the works had become the chief employer of labour and the focal point of the community. Agriculture, previously the principal source, came second in the economy. In 1889, the works was purchased by the 'Gwendraeth Tin Plate Company Ltd'.

The expansion of the industry was drastically checked in 1891 by the introduction of the Mackinley Tariff and the establishment behind it of a tinplate industry in the U.S.A., hitherto the market for three-quarters of British production, which was now almost a Welsh monopoly. Prices began to slump, production markedly declined, unemployment rose. The depression of the 1890s saw the works closed for almost four years, and its consequences were calamitous. The vicar, Rev. D. Daven Jones set up a soup kitchen in the Parish Room, whilst the Mayor set up a hardship fund. The works changed hands again in 1899 when it was bought by the Kidwelly Iron Sheet and Tin Plate Company. Within two years, however, the company went into voluntary liquidation. In 1904, the works became the property of the Kidwelly Tin Plate Company. The industry experienced a revival in trade under the control of John Thomas with almost continuous prosperity up to 1913. During the 1914-18 war, production was restricted and the industry stagnated. There was a brief post-war boom, but the expected return to prosperity was never to be fulfilled. The 1930s were for the tinplate workers their darkest time. There were prolonged periods of unemployment and the hope that prosperity would return faded with the loss of overseas markets. Production ceased in 1941 when the works was taken over by the Board of Trade and used for war storage purposes. Its conversion into a museum of the tinplate industry was begun in 1980 and today is the site of the Kidwelly Industrial Museum.

TARMACADAM INDUSTRY

In the 1920s-1930s two tarmacadam plants were in operation in the Kidwelly area. One was located at the town quay and the other at the Sidings, Mynydd-y-Garreg.

'The Pelican' at Kidwelly Quay, 1920s
(Photograph courtesy Author)

The plant at Mynydd-y-Garreg utilized stones hauled down from the local quarry. John Walters recalls starting work there as a young boy in 1934 and described it as being a dreadful place to work in, fraught with danger. The heat and fumes from the fires necessary to melt the tar, the noise from the crusher that shattered the quarry stones and the dust that invaded every nook and corner, all combined to constitute a very unhealthy workplace. Mr Walters, who still lives in the cottages opposite the Sidings, also recalls that you could write your name in the dust that covered all the furniture inside the cottages. About six people were employed at the plant.

The larger plant situated near the town quay imported stones by sea from Caldey Island. I quote from the *Llanelly Guardian*, May 1923: "The first cargo of stones from Caldey Island arrived at Kidwelly Quay for the Macadam Reed Stone Company, who have made the local quay their centre for distributing supplies to the county and district. The arrival of the vessel was witnessed by a large crowd at the quayside, and it is expected another three will dock during the week." Mr T. B. Gravell recalls the names of three of the vessels – 'The Pelican', 'Nautilus' and 'Elizabeth'. These vessels

Town councillors inspecting the new tarmac plant at the Quay, 1923. Note the steam powered lorry in the background.
(Photograph courtesy Peter Evans)

left the quayside loaded with coal for shipment to Laugharne and Llanstephan and returned with stones from Caldey Island. In the mid-1920s there were very few good road surfaces in the county and movement of cargo by sea was by far the easier method of conveyance. The end product – hot tarmacadam – was conveyed to various parts of the county by lorry. Some of the earlier lorries were steam powered and at various venues they would stop to take water on board. The plant closed down in the 1930s, yet another consequence of silt clogging up the estuary and harbour.

QUARRYING

Stephens & Co. Silica Quarries are believed to have started up early this century. Located high up at Mynydd-y-Garreg, limestone was being worked to the east while in the west there was an abundance of silica stone and sand. The 'New Quarry', referred to by the workers as 'The Deep', along with Tyfri Quarry were both silica workings, and Llyn Quarry was producing sand and clay.

Horses were used to haul drams to the rockface in the quarry and to transport stone by cart down to the Gwendraeth Valley Railway sidings in the early years. They were stabled on the site and an

Carts in the quarry, early 1900s
(Photograph courtesy M. R. C. Price)

ostler was appointed to look after them. The roads to Mynydd-y-Garreg were irregular and dilapidated and there was no lighting in the village until after World War I, all of which made the journey down to the sidings a perilous task to say the least. The fully laden carts would descend the steep hill with one wheel in the gutter so as to stabilise the speed and to avoid racing downhill out of control. Many accidents occurred at the sidings when tipping the loaded carts into the railway waggons as the horse and cart would often tip right over and land in the waggon with the stones. This happened mainly with stones from the sand quarry because the clay caused the stones to stick to the sides of the cart. The men would untack the frightened horse, leave the cart in the waggon to journey down to the brickworks where it was lifted out with a gantry. When hard frosts threatened in winter the blacksmith would fit ('oilon rhew') ice nails with spikes to the horse's hooves so there would be a grip on slippery surfaces. As there was so much wear on the hooves brought about by all the road work, the animals would be retired early and sold off to local farmers. They would be looked after on the farm and many lived to a ripe old age. An often repeated tale concerns a local contractor who liked his drink. His horse would automatically stop outside a country inn, viz the Prince of Wales, en route to Kidwelly. Landlady Mary Ann Price kept the inn open all day and charged one penny a pint. On this particular occasion this man drank more than usual and as the ale continued to flow a local wag went outside and turned the horse and cart around. The man finally emerged rather the worse for wear, shakily mounted the cart and drove off, only to end up where he had started from with his cartload of stone intact and undelivered. Yet another character who was overfond of the demon brew had a favourite saying: "they're always talking about my drinking, but never a word about my thirst."

The work was hard in the quarry in those early days – all stone had to be loaded by hand as there was no machinery. Boulders had to be broken down, since nothing over ¾ cwt in weight could be handled by the crusher down at the brickworks.

During blasting, men would be posted to close off the nearby road. On one occasion a boulder of approximately ten inch diameter flew through the air across the roadway, landing on 'Shop y Queen' with such force as to drive it through the roof. Fortunately, no one was injured.

A narrow gauge railway was laid in the quarry, and a self acting incline built to take the drams down to a siding alongside the

Quarrymen with the loco at Stephen's Quarry, 1925
(Photograph courtesy John Dennis Davies)

Gwendraeth Valley Railway. When the incline was opened all the schoolchildren turned out to see the first run of drams. Two bridges were built over the incline, one of which carried the date of construction, 1914. On several occasions the steel rope of the incline fractured and caused the dams to tip over and career down the steep slope, often landing in nearby gardens. At the head of the incline was a winding house with a brake, and the vitally important post of brakesman was held by Davey John Richards who enjoyed considerable respect. Other notable characters included Edgar Anthony, the locomotive driver from 1926 to 1939 and David Davies, the ganger in charge of track maintenance.

Buildings on the site included a blacksmith's shop, stables, workmen's cabin, an office, a stone-built engine shed and an iron store shed. For safety reasons the brick buildings had roofs of concrete, and the iron store shed roof was of concrete two inches thick.

SILICA BRICK MANUFACTURE

This chapter draws heavily on Chapter 7 of *The Gwendraeth Valleys Railway – Kidwelly to Mynydd-y-Garreg*, M. R. C. Price, 1998.

The mineral wealth of Mynydd-y-Garreg has over the years attracted many capitalists, who from time to time have been engaged in converting its silica stones into fire bricks and sand. The credit for pioneering this industry is given to William Edwards of Swansea, who is said to have constructed the first local brickworks in 1858. He was followed by Messrs. Frederick and Jenner who continued his business enterprise. In 1865 Messrs. Redford and Harries built a second brickworks, and were succeeded by Messrs. H. & H. E. Smart. A third was built by Alexander Young whilst a fourth was erected by Daniel Stephens.

Alexander Young
Young's choice of site for his brickworks was in Mynydd-y-Garreg near to a bank of five lime kilns he had erected earlier at Peny-mynydd Farm and adjacent to his standard gauge railway which ran down to the main line at Kidwelly. The foundations for the brickworks were laid by Young in 1900. In his speech he said:

> ". . . that whilst it was over 23 years since the foundation of the stone lime kilns, there was no better place in the principality for the erection of a silica brick works because here before us we have a mountain of silica sand and clay, and with a railway and all the material on the premises it looks good for the future."

To quote *Gwendraeth Valleys Railway*, M. R. C. Price:

> "Unfortunately this development soon became controversial. The year 1901 saw the climax of a complex dispute between the Kidwelly Corporation, which owned virtually all the limestone and silica on Mynydd-y-Garreg and certain producers, most notably Stephens & Co. Such was the ferocity of the argument in 1901 that the local press was moved to describe the row as the 'Kidwelly Silica Wars'. By now William Young appears to have been the most active figure in the business, and Alexander was becoming elderly."

Rev. Daven Jones writing in 1907, *Kidwelly – A History*, states Young was then deceased and the lime kilns at Penymynydd were out of use.
    M. R. C. Price, *Gwendraeth Valleys Railway*, continues:

> "The business continued however, trading after 1908 as A. Y.

Dinas Silica Brick & Lime Co.; most of the firm's output being refractory bricks used in the iron and steel industry. Aided no doubt by the onset of World War I, the company enjoyed some success and by 1917 plans were in hand to enlarge the works. In its original form the brickworks is believed to have had four kilns. The expansion provided for the construction of two more kilns, and another chimney stack, two crushers, a drying stove, pan mills, a brick press and a number of smaller items.

In 1922 at the time of the Great Western Railways takeover of the Gwendraeth Valleys Railway, the works – long known locally as 'Brickyard Young' – was said to be in the hands of the Amalgamated Dinas Silica Brick Co Ltd (note no longer the A. Y. Dinas Silica & Lime Co.). The same report indicates that the works were out of use, and that there was uncertainty when they would be active again. In the event it seems that the works never re-opened. It seems that the brickworks closed in 1921, but was kept intact for a few years in the hope of restarting production. The 1922 report suggests that rail traffic had then ceased. There is a local tradition that the very last bricks removed from the kilns were used in 1927 to complete the building of the Band Room for the once famous Mynydd-y-Garreg Silver Band."

Stephens & Co. Brickworks
Daniel Stephens was operating a brickworks near Kidwelly Railway Station in 1895 and a thriving extensive business was carried on there as can be seen from reports in the *Llanelly Guardian*.

OCTOBER 18TH 1895
Messrs. Stephens Silica Brick Works are going night and day to meet orders and shortly three steam boats are expected at Kidwelly Quay to take away cargoes to Belgium and the North of England. Some fifty men are employed, these ranging from quarrymen and hauliers down to the boys who carry the finished brick.

NOVEMBER 14TH 1895
Alfred Stephens co-owner of the brickworks complained that large vessels were unable to dock at the Quay and urged the Council to invest before local industries lost vital trade due to lack of shipping facilities. He continued: "Messrs. Stephens have never stopped work-

CONTRACTORS TO THE WAR OFFICE, ADMIRALTY,
INDIA OFFICE, AND MANY FOREIGN GOVERNMENTS.

SUPER SILICA BRICK
For Siemens Martin Furnaces.

PHOTOGRAPH FROM AN AEROPLANE OF

STEPHENS & CO.'S SILICA BRICK WORKS.
WORKS COVER OVER 9 ACRES.   KILN CAPACITY OVER 1½ MILLION BRICK.

Telephone:
No. 1.
Telegraphic Address:
" STEPHENS. KIDWELLY."

Codes:
A B C (4th & 5th Editions).
LEIBER'S.
MARCONI.

Other Grades of SILICA BRICK for all kinds of Furnaces.

Brickworks leaflet, 1920s
(Photograph courtesy Author)

ing since they started, and have shipped bricks to all parts of the world, even as far as China."

NOVEMBER 9TH 1902
Stephens & Co. have a growing trade in silica bricks and have landed a large contract to ship consignments to Glasgow Harbour.

Quoting from *The Gwendraeth Valleys Railway*, M. R. C. Price:

"In or about 1903 Stephens & Co. decided to expand the brick-

works on an open large green field site south of the South
Wales main line close to Kidwelly station. More kilns were
built and a siding laid in from the South Wales main line.
This was provided in 1904 to enable the works to receive
limestone, sand and clay from the Mynydd-y-Garreg district
and also coal, as well as to dispatch bricks to steelworks and
other customers some of whom were as far afield as Scotland.
At different dates no less than 20 kilns were built at this
works, but it is believed that a couple of the earlier small
kilns were demolished before the last three were built –
number 18, 19 and 20. At its greatest extent, therefore, this
brickworks had 18 operational, or potentially operational kilns,
and found success at a time when some other brick producers
like Youngs, were struggling."

The works continued to flourish making regular shipments of
cargoes from nearby Kymer's Dock connecting it with a short
tramroad. However, by 1914 Stephens & Co. no longer shipped
their consignments of bricks by sea as all traffic was by this time
carried by rail.

Details of the rolling stock at the works is taken from *The Gwendraeth Valleys Railway*, M. R. C. Price.

"In 1910 the brickworks company invested in a locomotive of
its own. This engine was given the name 'Barbara Cripps',
allegedly after the chief proprietor Sir Alfred Stephens' married daughter. During World War I a very similar saddle tank
locomotive was obtained and the 'Barbara Cripps' was sent
away to Lancashire. The new engine was named 'Broomhill'
after Sir Alfred Stephens' house. Some 30 years later the company purchased another similar engine which was named
very appropriately 'Sir Alfred'. Compared to its predecessors,
however, this engine did not have a long life. In 1965 Stephens'
Kidwelly brickworks was closed and the 'Sir Alfred' was
scrapped in August of the following year."

The brickworks at the height of its fame covered an area of over
nine acres with a kiln capacity of over 1½ million bricks. Amongst
its many customers were the War Office and many foreign governments. A leaflet distributed by the works shows the extensive grades
of silica brick manufactured, e.g.:

SUPER GRADE SILICA BRICK will stand 1800° cent.
For the Blocks, Roof and Walls of a Siemens
Martin Furnace.

SILICA "C" BRICK . . . will stand 1750° cent.
For Siemens Martin Furnace Jambs, Re-
generators, Steel Converters, Copper Works,
Glass Works, Gas Works, and all other
purposes where a very hard and tough
Silica Brick is required.

SILICA "B" BRICK . . . will stand 1700° cent.
For purposes where the Higher Grade Silica
Brick spall owing to the variations of temperature, and yet where a fairly high temperature has to be resisted.

STIGNIC "4" BRICK . . . will stand 1675° cent.
For lining Iron Cupolas, melting over 5
tons per hour, and for purposes where
variations of temperature are great.

STIGNIC "5" BRICK . . . will stand 1625° cent.
Far more refractory than Fireclay Brick and
yet will stand the variations of temperature. For Cupolas melting up to 5 tons per
hour, &c.

The following table affords a somewhat rough method
of estimating High Temperatures:

	Degrees Cent.
Just glowing in the dark.	525
Dark Red	700
Cherry Red	900
Bright Cherry Red	1,000
Orange	1,150
White	1,300
Dazzling White	1,500

The site of the brickworks has now been cleared, and is no more
than a field of scrub yielding graze for ponies.

6.

Sport

KIDWELLY TOWN BOWLING CLUB

Past
On the 26th May 1954 at a meeting held in the Town Hall, Kidwelly, chaired by the Mayor Ald. John Rees, J.P., it was resolved to form a Bowls Club "in order that full use of the new green at Parc Stephens may be made". Thus the Kidwelly Town Bowling Club was formed. At that meeting Mr T. W. Thomas, J.P. was elected President, Mr Emlyn Jones, Chairman and Captain, and Mr N. L. Johnson, Secretary. The membership fee was fixed at 5/- p.a. (25p) OAP 6d (2½p); today, a member in employment pays over £65 per annum and an OAP over £35 per annum.

Since that day of formation in 1954, Kidwelly Town Bowling Club has seen many changes of fortune – winning the top Division of the Llanelli and District Bowling League in 1978 and 1981, but are currently languishing in Division 3 of that same League. In the lists of previous winners of the various competitions held by the Llanelli League and other centres, the names of Kidwelly bowlers figure often but perhaps the most significant honour, that of representing one's own country, has fallen on two of our most eminent bowlers, i.e. Gwyn Griffiths, 1973-74-75, and Wynne John, 1977-78. Sadly, Gwyn is no longer with us, but Wynne plays on – a great servant of the Club as player and a former captain and chairman.

Presidents
During its existence the Club has had but five presidents:

1954-60	T. W. Thomas, J.P.
1961-79	Glyn Davies
1980-84	Roger Howells
1985-92	Derek Richards
1993-date	Neville Jones

Kidwelly Town Bowls Club, 1960
Back row: John Thorburn, John Morgan, Jack Lewis, Ron Walters, Ivor Youds,
Harry Jones, Vernon Wilkins. Middle row: D. T. Anthony, Glan Hughes,
Vaughan Jones, Ron Evans, Gavin Gravell, Gwyn Griffiths.
Front row: Delme Jones, Wyn John, Vincent Griffiths, Emlyn Jones.
(Photograph courtesy Jack Lewis)

Chairman

The position of Chairman has changed hands more frequently, N. L. Johnson for 13 years in the 50s, 60s and early 70s, and more recently:

1977-82	Ron Walters
1983-85	Mike Morgan
1986-96	Wynne John
1997-date	Will Morgan

Captains

1955-59	Emlyn Jones	1968	W. H. Jones
1960-63	Delme Jones	1969	W. O. Greville
1964	Vincent Griffiths	1970	Wynne John
1965	D. J. Anthony	1971	Gwyn Charles
1966	Glan Hughes	1972	John Thorburn
1967	John Morgan	1973	E. R. Thomas

1974	Gwyn Griffiths	1986-88	Wyn Samuel
1975	Ron Walters	1989-90	Mike Jones
1976	Eddie Abrahams	1991	Mike Morgan
1977	Gareth Thorburn	1992	Peter Jenkins
1978-79	Wynne John	1993	Glyn Collins
1980-81	Phil Jones	1994-97	Dennis Youds
1982-83	Keith Evans	1998-99	Keith Reeve
1984-85	Dennis Youds		

Kidwelly Town Bowling Club is indebted to all those named above and many more who have guided and served the Club during good and not so good years.

Present and Future
The Club has at Parc Stephens the use of one of the best bowling greens in the county, unhappily the pavilion and changing facilities do not match the quality of the playing surface. However, we have great hopes that the County Council will make funds available to improve the facilities. A start was made a few years ago but more remedial work remains before the home players and perhaps more importantly, visitors, can change in reasonable conditions.

Kidwelly Town Bowling Club currently plays in Division 3 of the Llanelli League and, whilst all the bowlers enjoy their bowls in whatever competitions they play, have every intention of climbing into higher divisions. To help the Club accomplish this objective and indeed continue as a viable bowling organisation in the Kidwelly area, it needs a continuing supply of new recruits, particularly younger members.

The Club stands looking to the future, the new millennium and later its Golden Anniversary, with great confidence – difficulties will be met and overcome and Kidwelly Town Bowling Club will prosper and grow.

KIDWELLY TOWN CRICKET CLUB

The history of Kidwelly Town Cricket Club has not been very well recorded, the early days are very vague. It is a fact that the club is over a hundred years old and started playing in a field near Muddlescwm Farm, and moved on to Cae Cow Parc now known as

Play in progress at Cae Cow Parc, now Parc Stephens, c.1909
(*Photograph courtesy William Beynon*)

Parc Stephens at around 1909. An unusual fixture held at Muddles-cwm was Kidwelly C.C. versus Yorkshire C.C., the reason for which is unclear. The first Captain of the club on record was J. H. Elias back in 1921. During the 1920s there were three cricket teams in Kidwelly: Stephens Silica Brick Co. Ltd. Cricket Club, the Bwrws Cricket Club, and Kidwelly Cricket Club. Other captains to follow were H. Hughes in 1926, A. Jones in 1930, S. Wilkins in 1933 followed by J. Morgan in 1934 and J. R. Green in 1937, where their head-quarters was the Pelican Hotel. Moving on to the 50s, Harold Rees took on the role in 1951 and Tal John in 1956.

A stalwart of the club in the 30s, 40s and 50s was Llew Rees. He was a good all-round cricketer and spent a large part of his life playing and working for the cricket club. Llew was Club Secretary for 25 years, Chairman for a number of years, and was honoured by being made Life Member of the cricket club. Llew Rees was known on the streets of the town by the nick-name Mr Cricket.

G. Thomas was captain in 1960 and 1961, William Morgan in 1963 and 1973, Gary Mumford in 1965 with Ivor John in 1968. The 1970s saw the club dominate the Carmarthenshire League under the cap-

KIDWELLY TOWN
CRICKET CLUB.

President—
Ald. Sir Alfred Stephens, J.P.

Vice-Presidents—
Thos. Anthony, Esq.
(London).
Capt. J. R. Green.
Lt.-Col. E. C. Jennings,
J.P., D.L., C.B.E.
Ald. T. W. Thomas.
Dr. P. C. Peace.
Dr. D. B. Davies.
Dr. A. J. Beckett.
Thos. Thomas, Esq.
John Rees, Esq.
R. C. Darch, Esq.
P. Paul, Esq.
Gerard Jones, Esq.
J. C. Jones, Esq.
W. C. Morgan, Esq.
Coun. J. Harries.
Mr. Antoniazzie.

Vice-Presidents—(contd.)
Coun. J. H. Rocke.
T. A. Morris, Esq.
W. J. Thomas, Esq.
J. Jones, Esq.

OFFICIALS.

Captain—
D. J. R. Morgan, Esq.

Vice-Captain—
C. G. Rees, Esq.

Hon. Treasurer—
Ald. John Morgan,
16, Water Street, Kidwelly.

Hon. Secretary—
H. Llew. Rees,
11, West Hill Crescent, Kidwelly.

Headquarters—Pelican Hotel.

Ground—Welfare Ground.

Committee—
Saml. Evans (Chairman).
Coun. David Davies
(Vice-Chairman).
Coun. Dd. Geo. Evans (Mayor).
Mr. Wm. Jenkins.
Mr. D. J. Hughes.
Mr. John Reynolds.
Coun. S. H. Evans, J.P.
Mr. J. Amos Jones, C.C.
Mr. Gwilym Hughes.
Mr. Thos. Gravell.
Mr. T. J. Edwards.
Mr. Harry Evans.
Mr. Geo. Dyke.
Mr. E. V. Jones.
Mr. Dd. Conniff.
Mr. T. J. Bevan.
Mr. Eddie Johns.
Mr. W. J. Parry.
Mr. Edgar Hughes.
Mr. D. R. John.
Mr. Elvet Fisher.
Ald. John Morgan.
Mr. H. Llew. Rees.

FIXTURES.

1937.	Opponents.	Ground.
May 1	Burry Port	home
8	Ystalyfera	away
15	Llanelly Steel	home
WM 17	Tenby	away
22	Morriston Town	home
29	County Offices, Carmarthen	home
June 5	Felinfoel	away
12	Skewen	home
19	Llanelly Steel	away
26	Morriston Town	away
30	(Wed.) Tenby	home
July 3	Skewen	away
10	Llanelly Stampers	away
17	Llandebie	home
24	Felinfoel	home
27	(Tues.) Llanelly Tuesdays	home
31	Haverfordwest Town	home
Aug.2	(B.H.) Hakin Milford-Haven	away
7	Ystalyfera	home
14	Burry Port	away
21	Haverfordwest Town	away
28	Llandebie	away
Sept. 4	Llanelly Stampers	home
11		home
14	(Tues.) Llanelly Tuesdays	home

Cricket Fixture Card – Season 1937
(Courtesy William Beynon)

taincy of Gwyndaf Jones who captained the side from 1974 to 1980 with the exception of 1976 when Peter Harries took over the role. Kidwelly were champions in 1974/5/6/7/8/9 and Cup winners in 1974/7/8/9 and 1980.

In 1981 the club decided to progress and joined the Morgannwg League, under the captaincy of David Walters. Instant success was achieved by winning the division 5 West title, followed in 1982 still under David Walters by winning division 4. 1983 saw the club moving into their new pavilion at Morfa Maen, and winning a further two trophies led by the late Phillip Case, they were division 3 and the M.C.L. Cup. The following year saw the side winning division 2 lead by Peter Williams. The club by now tried on a few occasions to join the South Wales Cricket Association, the premier league in Wales. They had been unsuccessful previously due to the ground at Morfa Maen not being considered up to the standard of the South Wales Cricket Association. The timing could not have been better, with the ground improvement and the new changing rooms having recently been built. In 1985, under the captaincy of Ted Hollands, the club made the move all players and club officers had been trying so hard to achieve, entry to division 5 of the S.W.C.A. The club managed to win the league in its first year, but unfortunately there was no promotion that year. In 1986 Ted Hollands led the side in winning the Llanelli Six-a-Side Tournament.

In 1987, under Gwyndaf Jones, the club were promoted as runners-up to division 4. The following year, 1988, saw club captain Peter Probert take the club to champions of division 4. 1989 still under the captaincy of Peter Probert saw them consolidate their position in division 3. In 1990 the club officers and committee in their search for success decided to employ a professional to see if the club could proceed further. A new era began, the first club professional, Aamir Ikram, joined the club. Aamir, a very experienced leg spin bowler, who, while playing for the club, represented his adopted country, Wales. Other international players that have played against the club were Ritchie Richardson and Keith Atherton of the West Indies. With the help of Aamir's professional attitude and hard work from the players and captain Gwyndaf Jones they became champions of division 3 in the same year. The club, not wanting to stand still, employed three further professionals in 1991, Mike Murphy from Gorseinon, Steve Wasserman from South Africa, and E. Soar from Dafen, followed later by Terry Marsh from South Africa.

Division two in the S.W.C.A. was the highest level the club had ever played and unfortunately fell back to their present position in division 5. In order from 1992 to 1999 the captains were: Ammir Ikram, Ammir Ikram, Gwyndaf Jones, Gwyndaf Jones, Jarrod Davies, Jarrod Davies, Steve Wasserman and David Walters.

KIDWELLY TOWN AFC

Kidwelly, always being a 'rugby' town, never gave soccer any credibility, so when a side was re-formed and entered into the Carmarthenshire League in 1959, under the guidance of Ken Barry (local Stationmaster) Chairman; Aelwyn Jones, Secretary; and energetic committee members Bill Toy, Raymond Collins, John Owen, Tommy Davies, Henderson Samuel, Walter (Jock) Turnbull, George Turner, Dai Hussey, Trevor Jones and Leighton Bowen, Club President Mr Glyn Davies and trainer Hubert Baker, nothing was ever expected of them other than when they would 'fold'.

The team played on the brickyard field, travelling down to the pitch from their headquarters based in the Castle Hotel.

After an uneventful beginning, with a side made up mainly of young exuberant players, the team found themselves near the bottom of the table at the end of the first season. A much more balanced side developed in the following year, and with the addition of experienced players in the form of John Pearce, Roy and Delme Davies, mid-table respectability was achieved.

The next season 1962-63 saw the birth of 'footballing success' for Kidwelly – this year the blend of youth and experience with two years of spadework behind them, had progressed into a really useful Cup side. Although no more than holding their own in the League, their cup performances were exceptional and they were well deserved finalists. However, meeting Porthyrhyd in the final was akin to scaling a mountain as they were the odds-on favourites for the tournament. Porthyrhyd, who paraded the skills of a 17-year-old Barry John in their line up (later to distinguish himself on the rugby field with Cardiff and Wales), were rather shocked to be held to a draw in the first encounter. Kidwelly fans, starved of any sporting success for so long (in their history), came out in their droves for the replay at Stebonheath Park. They were not to be disappointed for the Town ran out 2-0 winners, thanks to fine goals scored by their

Kidwelly Town AFC
Carmarthenshire League Cup Winners 1962/63 Season
Reading from top left: Linesman, Trevor Jones, Bill Toy, Edmund Gravell,
Ray Foligno, Derek Fisher, Tommy Davies, John Pearce, Dai Hussey,
Gordon Reynolds, John Owens, Raymond Collins, Referee.
Seated front row, left to right: Tony Thorburn, Harry Reynolds, Michael Hughes,
Aelwyn Jones, Clive Davies (Captain), John Thomas, Idwal Roberts, Wyn Hughes.
Bottom row: Delme Davies.
(Photograph courtesy Lord Nelson Inn)

captain Clive Davies (who also went on to a successful rugby career with Llanelli).

After this epic Cup victory, records of the later performances of the team have been lost and one is not sure when the team disbanded.

In 1984 the Football Club was re-formed when three local men on their way to play for another team posed the question – "Why not form our own team?" The three involved – Walter (Jock) Turnbull, Malcolm Morris and Michael Fitzpatrick, decided to find out what interest there would be in the town to form a football team. Pleased with the response they went ahead and a committee was set up with Mr Huw Gravell, President; John Thomas, Chairman; Michael Fitzpatrick, Secretary; and Peter Gower, Treasurer. Their first problem was where to play their home matches as renovation work was badly needed to the practice pitch in Parc Stephens. This was solved when Pembrey AFC allowed home league fixtures to be played on their grounds. The next problem to manifest was lack of football kit and this was resolved when Porth Tywyn Suburbs helped out by selling one of their spare sets. The Club was reborn with the appointments of Mike Evans as team manager and Walter Turnbull as captain.

The first league game was played versus New Dock Wolves at Llanelli with the team off to a flying start by winning by 4 goals to 2. This proved to be a very successful beginning with the team finishing 3rd in the League. The following year, 1985-86, Kidwelly Town played home matches at Parc Stephens where they were instantly successful and won their first trophy. Walter Turnbull, re-elected captain, steered the team to win the Carmarthenshire League Division 3 Championship. Player of the Year was goalkeeper Terry Williams who only conceded 16 goals in all games played during that season.

The Club's success on the field resulted in a new post being created for the 1986-87 season – that of fixture secretary – a position filled by Michael Fitzpatrick. A notable change to the officials was the appointment of Andrew Lloyd as treasurer, a position he holds to this day. This again proved to be a successful season with the team reaching the final of the Challenge Cup. The surge of interest in the Club led to a reserve team being formed.

The new Club's most successful season came in 1988-89 with both first and second teams winning their respectful divisions. The senior side lifting the Carmarthen League Division 2 Championship Trophy and the second string winning the Division 3 Reserve Championship. As the Club entered the nineties the position of club secretary became a real problem, a post that was continually changing hands. For the 1991-92 season Kevin Davies took up the post and brought much needed stability to the Club and he continues to hold the position of secretary today.

The Club was now going from strength to strength and a permanent base for the team was essential. This difficulty was overcome when the Club returned to the Lord Nelson Hotel which remains the team Clubhouse. The team were to win more trophies, the Carmarthen & District Football Festival in 1993 and the Gwendraeth Valley Cup in 1995. There was disappointment in the 1994-95 season when the team was relegated to Division 2. However, the following season they were promoted to Division 1 as champions of Division 2, beating Abergwili by 7 goals to 2 to lift the trophy.

Team Captains

	First Team	Reserve Team
1962-63	Clive Davies	
1984-85	Walter Turnbull	
85-86	Walter Turnbull	
86-87	Walter Turnbull	Malcolm Morris
87-88	Walter Turnbull	Malcolm Morris
88-89	Mike Griffiths	Malcolm Morris
89-90	Kelvin Thomas	
90-91	Peter Evans	
91-92	Peter Evans	
92-93	Peter Evans	
93-94	Paul Evans	
94-95	Paul Evans	
95-96	Paul Evans	Ray Johns
96-97	Wyn Phillips	Kevin Davies
97-98	Paul Evans	Kevin Davies
98-99	Patrick Lilley	Kevin Davies

KIDWELLY RUGBY CLUB

The turn of the century is a watershed in that it provides a suitable period to reflect on the previous hundred years and anticipate the developments of the next. The turn of the nineteenth century had seen the existence of a Rugby Club in Kidwelly for some twenty years, as the first historical records confirm that the Club was founded in 1879-80 and that Kidwelly was not alone in having a club. There were by 1880 some thirty clubs in existence and reflected communities that were identified by coal mining and other heavy industries. The turn of the millennium in 1899 saw some seventy clubs in being, although this did not take into account a myriad of other organizations, many of which were casual and temporary which played rugby with local rivalries generating fierce encounters, many of which remain in the form of local derbies played with the current national league structure and administered by the Welsh Rugby Union.

As in many other communities the historic evidence for the existence of rugby football clubs is somewhat sketchy. The forcing purpose was to play the game and although administration did exist there were few written documents to illuminate the establishment

Kidwelly RFC v. Felinfoel at Gorseinon RFC Ground, 1947/48 Season
Back row, reading left to right: Danny Mitchell (Chairman), Referee,
Aelwyn Jones (Treasurer), Anthony Lewis, Will Roberts, Gough Williams,
Eddie Parry, Doug Rees, Hubert Evans, Haydn Rees, David Howells (Secretary),
Tommy Edwards (Trainer). Middle row: Jack Gravell, Derrick Gower,
Ron John (Captain), Alec Lewis, Eddie Morris, Haydn Thomas.
Front row: John Jones, Gwyn Gravell.

(Photograph courtesy Kidwelly Rugby Club)

of the Club. Despite the paucity of a rugby archive there is sufficient data to confirm the success of the Club in its early days and it was even then, some ten years after its founding, a source of talent for larger clubs, particularly Llanelli. The pattern of clubs, limited by the size and wealth of its community, has remained as a nursery for larger clubs whose wealth and status distinguished them from the many formal and informal organizations committed to fostering the game of rugby in Wales. As early as 1890 Stephen Thomas, who had been born in Kidwelly and who had played for the town, played for Wales against both England and Scotland, and a year later represented Wales against Ireland.

There is evidence to suggest that the growth of the Club was hampered by social and economic forces at the turn of the century and there was a re-launch of the Club in 1913 and was known as the Castle Club. The early tradition in Wales was to give clubs nicknames rather than take the name of the town or community. Kidwelly was known as the Red and Greens and its nickname was the

'Moonlights'. Its restructuring was due probably to a financial debt although the records are obscure. The most significant feature of the re-launch was that it pre-empted later developments in that it was more than a rugby club and in truth was an athletics club, catering for both soccer and hockey, although no changing facilities were available and players changed by the side of the hedge and supported the Club by individual contributions. The First World War disrupted the game in Wales and the Welsh Football Union (the forerunner of the WRU) encouraged players to enlist, buoyed by the belief that the war would be over quickly. Some fifty men volunteered from Kidwelly and the clubs in Wales were advised to cease playing; the decision in 1916 to create a conscript army made it extremely difficult to continue rugby in the town. However, by 1921 Kidwelly Juniors played in the final of the Lady Howard Cup against Richard Thomas Juniors and lost by 8 points to 6, although the winning try was allegedly scored after the ball had been minored. So disgusted was a Kidwelly player that he is claimed to have sold his medal immediately after the game. In 1930 the Kidwelly Juniors won the first trophy for the Club when the XV won the Llanelli & District League, having beaten Felinfoel and Bynea in the semi-final and final. The matches were also important because the Juniors played in green (the current alternative colour of the Club) and the senior side known as Kidwelly Harlequins played in black and amber which has remained their traditional jerseys.

The Club had acquired an administrative base with Constitutions and a President. In 1931-32 the President was Sir Alfred Stephens, the industrialist who had developed Kidwelly Silica Brick Works, which employed a significant number of the players. Sir Alfred donated Parc Stephens to the town to be used by the Rugby Club for the purposes of rugby football and which today remains a charitable trust dedicated to the pursuit of rugby in the community. It was the vision and generosity of individuals like Sir Alfred that enables many communities in Wales to acquire playing facilities and establish rugby football on a much more secure basis.

World War Two inevitably disrupted the game throughout Wales. The 1939-40 season ended on 3rd September with the outbreak of war and the Emergency Act banned the gathering of crowds in any place for entertainment and sport, and on 5th September the Welsh Rugby Union resolved to suspend its activities for the duration of the war. The initial decisions had been based on the experience of the First World War but it became apparent that sport in particular boosted morale and the restrictions were lessened. After the Battle of Britain and the removal of the threat of invasion, rugby began to be played again. For six years the WRU had ceased to be in control of rugby and it was not until September 1945, when club games were resumed, did rugby fall under the control of the WRU. There is some evidence that a few rugby matches were played during the war years, particularly with the RAF base in Pembrey, and the organization of the Club continued through the efforts of individuals. It was this continuity that enabled the Club to be admitted as full members of the Union in 1948 and began to play in the West Wales Rugby Football Union's League and Cup competitions.

It was during the sixties that the competitive zeal of the Club gained its rewards. The playing record was supplemented in 1966 when the Club acquired its own clubhouse by leasing the Castle Hotel from Felinfoel Brewery. The property was substantially renovated and the former British Legion Hall was demolished and the main hall of the club constructed. The clubhouse has been a major factor in nurturing community spirit as it is used by many organizations in support of their activity and reflects the central role of the Club in the communal life of the town. In 1965 the frustration of failing to gain trophies in the highly competitive West Wales competition was finally expurgated. The defeat of both Pontardulais (ending a 65 match unbeaten run) and Loughor in the final of the League Championship, and a repetition of the achievement in the following season established the Club as a formidable competitive force which was to auger well for the National Leagues which finally replaced the West Wales League Championship. The Club was to win the League Championship on four separate occasions. It was also successful in the Challenge Cup competition, winning in 1972-73 and again in 1979-80. The impact of the Club on the West Wales League was sealed with three triumphs in the Presidents' Club played between the winners of the Championship and Cup competitions. On three occasions in 1969-70, 1975-76 and finally in 1979-80 the Club was triumphant. It is significant that in its centenary year it won the West Wales Challenge Cup as a fitting commemoration of a century of rugby football played in the town.

The Centenary Year was also remarkable when the Club embarked on its most pioneering venture when it toured Canada and chartered a Boeing 707 to visit Toronto, Hamilton, London and played against teams which were the leading clubs in the Ontario Rugby Football Union. The Club also hosted a return visit by Toronto Welsh and apart from the rugby the tour culminated in a Max Boyce concert in the Club, which informed the public of the folk status that the performer has created based on his passion for the game in Wales. The international side of the Club's activities have continued with visits to Czechoslovakia, Spain and Portugal and to Dublin with Terenure College. Perhaps the international perspective found greatest expression with the visit of the Moscow XV to Kidwelly long before the era of Glasnost and the scant attention paid to political commissar who accompanied the team. Perhaps the visit planted the germ of dissonance in the minds of the Russian visitors who were mystified by the freedom of the west and the subdued role of authority in the affairs of the community.

The 1990s saw the most dramatic change in the structure of the game in Wales. The decline in the standard of Welsh rugby and the supremacy of the Southern Hemisphere led to the belief that a reorganization of rugby in Wales was necessary. The WRU agreed to introduce a National League structure involving the top clubs in Wales although it was to be expanded to include all members of the WRU. Kidwelly qualified for the inaugural National League following its achievements in Division 'A' of the West Wales League and despite a less than consistent record of achievement won Division 5 of the League in 1995-96 and was promoted to Division 4. The National League was further characterised by the introduction of a fully professional game following a decision of the International Rugby Board which has produced a series of changes not contemplated when the original decision was made. It was self-evident early in the professional era that the financial basis of the game in Wales had altered considerably and the demands of players' contracts and the increased mobility of players between clubs has thwarted traditional loyalties and balance of playing strength. It is increasingly apparent that clubs which do not have significant financial backing will find the demands of the modern game difficult to satisfy and the modifications of the game at a global effect have serious impacts on the local game, which is unable to meet the escalating costs of creating a strong squad of players. The introduction of the European Cup, the global coverage of the game on TV, the restrictions imposed by TV companies on scheduling, the prospect of a British League, Super Twelve competitions, all suggest that the game is truly a world sport and local national unions have to react to sustain its place in the ultimate competition of all the World Cup.

These structural changes place great emphasis on investment in rugby by clubs, and Kidwelly has pioneered schoolboy rugby at all levels with its junior section, and as the long-term strategy to fuel the increasing demands for talent and skills, as the game demands higher levels of appeal to attract and sustain a global market and attract sponsors. In addition to its junior section Kidwelly RFC has long supported a Youth XV and a Harlequin XV, and is able to offer rugby in one club from the age of 6 or 7 until retirement. As one approaches the third millennium the challenges manifest themselves in greater relief each season as the changes are introduced at all levels. There is an obvious threat to clubs which represent single communities as the scale of reform needed places an emphasis on larger organizations which can only be met by mergers and acquisitions. It is this challenge that Kidwelly RFC has identified as the task for the Millennium and one which it is confident of meeting.

Kidwelly RFC Captains

1880/81	J. H. Truscott	1902/03	
1881/82	J. H. Truscott	1903/04	Tom Davies
1882/83	J. H. Truscott	1904/05	
1883/84	J. H. Truscott	1905/06	
1884/85	J. H. Truscott	1906/07	
1885/86	Dan Davies	1907/08	Saunders Davies
1886/87	John Thomas	1908/09	W. A. Davies
1887/88	Dan Davies	1909/10	Jack Lloyd
1888/89	Dan Williams	1910/11	D. R. Wild
1889/90	W. Williams	1911/12	
1890/91	David Williams	1912/13	
1891/92	W. Davies	1913/14	W. G. Lewis
1892/93	David Thomas	1914/15	⎫
1893/94		1915/16	⎬ World War 1
1894/95		1916/17	⎭
1895/96		1917/18	
1896/97		1918/19	Jim Lloyd
1897/98		1919/20	D. Y. Lewis
1898/99		1920/21	W. J. Roberts
1899/1900	Tom Powell	1921/22	Tom Stephens
1900/01	Will Fisher	1922/23	T. R. Lewis
1901/02		1923/24	Tom Evans

1924/25	Tom Evans	1962/63	Bruce McNally
1925/26	T. R. Lewis	1963/64	Hywel Rees
1926/27	T. R. Lewis	1964/65	Hywel Rees
1927/28	Glan Marks	1965/66	John Antoniazzi
1928/29	Frank John	1966/67	Hywel Rees
1929/30	Sammy Nicholas	1967/68	Ken Denman
1930/31	Ritchie Williams	1968/69	Allan Denman
1931/32	Will Morgan	1969/70	Marlston Morgan
1932/33	Frank John	1970/71	Marlston Morgan
1933/34	Will Thomas	1971/72	Freddie Bevan
1934/35	Arthur Bevan	1972/73	Harry Reynolds
1935/36	Willie Hughes	1973/74	Colin John
1936/37	Frank Thomas	1974/75	Peter Johns
1937/38	Evan Thomas	1975/76	Alan Williams
1938/39	Jack Lewis	1976/77	Ian Davies
1939/40	Gwyn Griffiths	1977/78	Alan T. Williams
1940/41	Eddie Morris	1978/79	Alan T. Williams
1941/42	⎫	1979/80	John Chapman
1942/43	⎬ World War 2	1980/81	John Chapman
1943/44	⎪	1981/82	John Chapman
1944/45	⎭	1982/83	Peter Harries
1945/46	Gwyn Griffiths	1983/84	Peter Williams
1946/47	Anthony Lewis	1984/85	Peter Williams
1947/48	Ron John	1985/86	Raymond Williams
1948/49	Anthony Lewis	1986/87	Peter Williams
1949/50	Peter Kingsbury	1987/88	Peter Williams
1950/51	Emlyn Badham	1988/89	Stephen Williams
1951/52	Bernard Price	1989/90	Stephen Williams
1952/53	Harry Jones	1990/91	Peter Williams
1953/54	Eddie Morgan	1991/92	Stephen Williams
1954/55	David Thomas	1992/93	Charlie Jacob
1955/56	David Thomas	1993/94	Peter Morris
1956/57	Harry Jones	1994/95	Stephen John
1957/58	Richie Rowlands	1995/96	Peter Morris
1958/59	David Thomas	1996/97	Les Mathias
1959/60	David Reynolds	1997/98	Craig Thomas
1960/61	Bruce McNally	1998/99	Martin King
1961/62	Dennis Youds		

7.

Legends

The remotest antiquity of Kidwelly is attested by some of the place names handed down through the ages to the present time. Among these names are 'Y Maenllwyd Mawr' and 'Allt Cunedda'.

'Y MAENLLWYD MAWR' (THE GREAT HOARY STONE)

Located on the old road leading eastwards on an eminence about half a mile from the town there is an enclosure referred to as 'Y Maenllwyd Mawr' (The Great Hoary Stone). However, there is no trace, as one would expect in a field under cultivation, of the hoary stone, probably a megalithic monument, commonly called a *cromlech* whereby the enclosure got its name.

Tradition has it that this was the location of an old Christian Church 'Llanfihangel' (the Church of St Michael), whilst a spring flowed into a well chamber called 'Ffynnon Fihangel' (St Michael's Well) in a neighbouring field. A short while ago I walked the large field known as 'Y Maenllwyd Mawr' and found it littered with stones and stone shards, whereas neighbouring fields were found to be relatively clean. Many of these stones were cut and dressed, indicating that they had been used in some kind of building. During a discussion with landowner Mr Daniel Gravell, he told me: "it was a field that did not want to be ploughed and that it had been a costly exercise in terms of ploughshare breakages and general wear and tear on farm machinery."

'ALLT CUNEDDA' (THE HILL OF CUNEDDA)

'Allt Cunedda' is the name given to a hill north-east of the town. Cunedda was a ruler of the Brythons in Wales AD 500. He became ruler over Gwynedd and his descendants, the 'sons of Cunedda', made themselves rulers over other and various parts of the country. Allt Cunedda is the site of a fortress said to have been built by Cunedda or one of his sons. It can be seen in the Ordnance Survey Map of 1842 that the spot is marked 'Ancient Fortress'. Excavations bear testimony to the probability of the existence at one time of a somewhat extensive fortification in this place.

Excavations in 1850 of a mound called 'Banc Benisel' revealed 2 ft below the original surface, a hexagonal flat stone, measuring 8'4" x 7'0" and 12-15 inches thick. Underneath the stone there was found an almost entire human skeleton, the head damaged as if hit by a stone from a sling. The teeth were entire (indicating prime of life). There were no ornaments or weapons. Position was north-east to south-west with the head to the north-east.

A second mound situated further to the east of the camp was opened in 1850, and this appeared to have been a general repository for bodies of the slain which had been burned, and ashes and earth were mixed in a heap. This tumulus has since been levelled and its exact position is not known.

In the year 1881, William Williams ploughing a field near 'Banc Benisel' came upon the remains of a stone cist, 4 stones crushed in. He made use of them by placing two at his farmyard gate and two at the western hedge of the field.

LORE AND LEGEND

"Many of the legends, folk stories and folklore of Wales were collected in the seventies and eighties of the last century – meeting and discussing with old people who had heard their stories from even older people," writes D. Parry Jones, *Welsh Legends and Fairy Lore*, 1953. He continues:

"When an elderly man of 80 or more relates his tales as heard in his early youth from men equally as old, a period of nearly a century and a half is spanned, and takes one back to the early decade of the eighteenth century. And Wales did not lose out much in the way of communal games, national customs, habits of life, lore and legend for another hundred years. By that time Methodism had become so powerful and influential that legends and such like began to die out, where they were not directly attacked, and a new Wales emerged in which religion, the respectability that went with it, the striving to 'get on', and the pursuit of culture, became the main concerns of the people. Not only were the old lore and customs held to be unworthy of an emancipated and enlightened age, they were also condemned as belonging to a past that was ignorant and superstitious, and in bondage to sin. They were, too, contrary to the teaching of the gospels which gives no place in the system to the existence of fairies, goblins and ghosts, but rather to the devil and his wicked angels."

The following verse is from *Legends and Folk Lore of South Wales*, Hilda A. E. Roberts, 1931:

"Yr hen ŵr llwyd o'r cornel
    Gan ei dad a glywodd chwe del
A chan ei dad fe glywodd yntau
    Ac ar ei ôl my gofias innau".

"The old grey man of the corner
    Of his father heard a story
Which from his father he had heard
    And after them I have remembered".

A HAUNTED BRIDGE

The Ghost of Pont-y-Gwendraeth
There was an old belief among the Welsh people in former times that the spirit of a 'suicide' was doomed to walk the earth as a punishment. The following is a well known local legend.

Sir Elidir Ddu was Lord of Kidwelly who had two sons – Griffith and Rhys – and a beautiful daughter Nest.

The Crusades had been proclaimed and Elidir was preparing to depart accompanied by his younger son Rhys. The elder son, Griffith, and Nest, the only daughter, remained at home in Kidwelly Castle, as well as another fair young lady whose name was Gwladys, a niece of Sir Elidir and cousin to Nest. At this time Nest was in love with a handsome young Norman, named Sir Walter Mansel. Gwladys was also in love with him but the young man was true to Nest. Griffith loved Gwladys but she did not like him as she wanted Sir Walter. This complicated the whole situation.

Before leaving for the Holy Land, Elidir had forbidden the young Norman entry to the house and the young lady's brother – Griffith – guarded the place against him, but the sanguine lover found means of meeting the fair Nest in the country around. But the jealous Gwladys watched Nest and found out the place of rendezvous (which was Pont-y-Gwendraeth) and she informed Griffith of it. Griffith was in love with Gwladys but she had snubbed him. Now, however, in order to use him as an accomplice in her revenge on Nest, she flattered him with feigned kindness and wrought him up to such a pitch of fury against the Norman that he agreed to join her in destroying the young lover by enlisting the help of a bad fellow called Merig Manteg to carry out the evil deed.

The next meeting place of the lovers was by some means ascertained to be a bridge over the tidal portion of the Gwendraeth, and as Sir Walter came forward to greet his lady love an arrow whistled from a reed bed and pierced his side. The villain Merig, then rushed from his hiding place and before the very eyes of Nest, hurled Sir Walter's body into the rushing water. The young lady, overcome with horror, gave a wild shriek of despair and plunged in after the hapless knight.

After this, the villain Merig was haunted by Nest's spirit, and on one occasion she told him that her spirit was doomed to walk the earth as a punishment for her suicide unless a marriage took place between one of her father's descendants and a member of the Mansel family, and until that time she would appear on Pont-y-Gwendraeth to give warning of the approaching death of every member of the family. From that day the bridge became known as Pont yr Ysbryd Gwyn (The Bridge of the White Spirit). For generations after, a white lady occasionally appeared giving utterance to a wild unearthly shriek and vanished.

A sequel to this tale occurred centuries later.

In 1775 Mr Rhys, a lineal descendant of Rhys Ddu of Kidwelly Castle (a magistrate), was returning one evening from the Quarter Sessions when he was startled at seeing a white figure flit rapidly across the bridge, disappearing into the water. His horse trembled and refused to go on. Mr Rhys thought of the ghost story and the prediction, and riding toward Kidwelly noticed a large crowd gathered. He heard that a shocking murder had been committed, the victim being a poor old woman. He entered the cottage and discovered a small portion of a man's coat sleeve lying upon the bed. On enquiry, he found it belonged to 'Will Manteg'. Will was arrested and confessed, and was hanged on Pembrey Mountain, while to still further strengthen the prediction Mr Rhys was informed that day of the death of his brother Arthur of the R.N. who was drowned at sea. Also he learned of his mother's death, Lady Mansel of Iscoed, who was burnt to death at Kidwelly.

The bridge is known locally as 'Spudders Bridge'. It is believed that the original form was 'Spriter's Bridge' from an old English word 'Sprite' which means apparition. This word is probably connected with the Welsh word 'Ysbryd' (ghost). In former times the bridge was known as 'Pont yr Ysbryd Gwyn' (The Bridge of the White Spirit).

THE BATTLE OF MAESGWENLLIAN

A narrative of Kidwelly town would be totally incomplete without a recollection of the tale of Gwenllian, a Welsh heroine, who led an army against the Normans. Giraldus Cambrensis, the chronicler, writing sixty years after the event, said: "she marched like the Queen of the Amazons leading her army." No woman had led an army into battle for a thousand years – that is to say since the days of Boadicea.

Gwenllian, reputedly a beautiful princess, was the daughter of Gruffudd ap Cynon, King of Gwynedd. The 12th century heroine married Gruffudd ap Rhys, Prince of Deheubarth (South West Wales), and had four sons named Meredudd, Morgan, Maelgwyn and Rhys.

When King Henry I died in 1135, the whole of South Wales was under Norman control. In 1136 the Welsh rose in rebellion and in a battle which took place near Loughor the enemy was defeated and 500 Normans were killed. Gruffudd ap Rhys decided that the time was now ripe to strike again to recover his lost dominions. He rode north seeking reinforcements. While he was away Maurice de Londres, Lord of Kidwelly and Carnwyllion, decided to counter-attack. Gwenllian gathered her forces, put herself at the head of a Welsh army and marched to attack the town and castle.

On a hillside north of Kidwelly to the west of the Gwendraeth Fach river, Maurice de Londres lined up his soldiers ready for battle. To this day the area is known as Kingswood. Princess Gwenllian led the Welsh forces into battle accompanied by two of her sons, Morgan and Maelgwyn. A bloody battle took place in a field to the east of the river preceding Gwenllian's capture and the defeat of her forces. The Normans beheaded the Welsh princess and one of her sons – Morgan – was also killed. The area is known even to this day as Maes Gwenllian (Gwenllian's field).

Gwenllian's death caused a bitterness that lasted for centuries. Long indeed did the Normans rue the cruel stroke that beheaded the brave princess. Blood ran like water and steel flashed like lightning to avenge the foul deed. However, Gwenllian's death was not entirely a disaster, as her bravery served to inspire a nation and brought about a close bond between the Welsh princes and led to a resurgence to push the Normans out of Wales.

Her death was avenged within a matter of months. Her husband and brothers defeated a huge Norman army at Crug Mawr near Cardigan and drove the Normans out of Ceredigion, which remained under Welsh control for 150 years.

Half a century later, Gwenllian's son, Rhys ap Gruffudd, who was only four years old when she died, won back his father's kingdom and ruled the whole of South Wales. Today, almost 900 years after the famous battle, Gwenllian's name still evokes local pride, and she will never be forgotten.

THE HEADLESS GHOST

There are many tales of the headless ghost of Kidwelly – here follows one.

Gwenllian was a Welsh princess, a local heroine who led an army against the Normans. In an epic battle in the year 1136 Gwenllian's forces were defeated – one of her sons was killed, she was captured and beheaded.

For centuries following on from this criminal act, the headless ghost of a woman was seen wandering the battlefield (Maes Gwenllian) Gwenllian's Field, the banks of the castle and the area within the old town barbican.

One moonlit night two local men out walking caught sight of the ghost. Had either of them been alone, doubtless he would have made a hasty retreat to the safety of his home. However, neither of the men wanted to show the other he was afraid, so they held their ground as the apparition drew near. Finally, one of the men ventured to ask the woman – "Why are you wandering around this area so late at night?" "Please, please help me," she answered, "I cannot rest until I have found my head." For three nights these two men searched the area and eventually found the missing severed part.

Gwenllian's ghost was never seen again, wandering the slopes of Mynydd-y-Garreg, nor the area around the castle.

THE SPECTRE OF THE CASTLE

Stories of ghostly figures in and around the castle have been abundant down the ages, and legendary tales suggest that on dark and murky nights the ghosts of Owain Glyndŵr and Princess Gwenllian can be seen inside and in the vicinity of the castle. In fact 'a ghostly presence' is the experience described of recent sightings and reported on by local townspeople and other visitors to the castle. The area within the confines of the gatehouse in particular has been the venue of a number of these apparitions. At this location one can look down into a large bare pit, the castle's main dungeon.

Some people claim to have observed a luminous figure that seems to float on air and flits around while others describe the spectre of a soldier. This ghostly form is said to have been seen within the castle grounds but more often is portrayed as standing on the battlements as though on sentry duty. The accurate and constant description given by people claiming to have seen this soldier is quite uncanny – tall, upright posture, head apparel of a helmet, long flowing robe and holding a staff or similar weapon.

THE PHANTOM STAGECOACH

There are countless stories relating to a phantom stagecoach having been seen on dark and dreary nights, crashing along the road between Four Roads and Mynydd-y-Garreg situated on the outskirts of Kid-

welly. Many local people claim to have seen a coach and four which suddenly appear out of the darkness – a ghostly apparition that fills the inky black night with a thundering of horses hooves and the champing, clanking noise of wheels on the road – and then disappear into the dingy darkness just as mysteriously.

One of the tales is described by a local couple travelling in their car on this stretch of road on a dark, bleak mid-winter evening. Having left behind them the lights of Mynydd-y-Garreg, they continued their journey steadily towards Four Roads. On negotiating a sharp bend, they perceived a dimly lit object ahead and as this was a very dark section of the road they were uncertain as to what exactly was coming toward them. Moments later, with a suddenness that startled them, they saw a coach and horses racing into their path. There was very little hope of avoiding a collision as the coach was by now almost on top of them. The couple were totally panic stricken and the car driver slammed his foot on the brakes. In the car headlights they saw clearly a team of four white horses hurtling out of the darkness, and two men seated on the coach. The driver wore a tall dark hat and was furiously cracking a whip over the horses and urging them to race even faster. The occupants of the car were very frightened (to say the least) by the thundering of hooves and the clanking noise of iron clad wheels on the road. The coach was large and dark, and they both were similarly aware of the polished lamps which gleamed in the car headlights. The car was at a standstill and the pair braced themselves for the inevitable collision, but to their utter amazement the coach and horses seemed to drive right through them. A mixture of emotions overwhelmed them causing them to be completely dumbstruck and gripped with an icy coldness.

Turning their heads in fear to look through the rear window of the car, all they saw was the blackness of the night – as suddenly as it had appeared so had the ghostly coach vanished. The clonking, champing and thundering noise had stopped, the car engine had stalled and the occupants of the car were only too well aware of an eerie silence. All they could hear was the thumping beat of their hearts pounding in their chests.

They eventually arrived home, shaken but unharmed by their ghostly encounter – an experience they will never ever forget.

Here is another tale: A young lad from Kidwelly was courting a girl who lived in the village of Four Roads. He recounts how on leaving his girl friend's home late one night he faced a three mile walk along a quiet country road, a journey he had made many times. The road was deserted at this late hour and he knew that for a mile or so he would see nothing but dark hedgerows before reaching the first of several cottages dotted along the way. Despite the frosty air, he was pleased that the weather was dry. Soon, however, he found the walk had become a hard slog because of the strong headwind he was directly walking into. He found the going much easier with head bowed to the ground but had difficulty in keeping to the roadway in such pitch darkness.

He had barely covered half a mile of his journey when he lifted his head to see the way forward and in the distance observed a glimmer of light. He decided he would have to keep as close to the hedgerow as he could in order to be well clear of the oncoming vehicle. On lifting his head into the strong wind a second time, he was surprised to find that the faint light was still some way off – 'must be a cyclist' he surmised.

Shortly afterwards a noise exploded out of the silence of the night with an impact that startled and frightened him. There, hurtling toward him and riding the crown of the road was a stagecoach, dark and eerie with a faint but glowing light on one side. Seated on top was a driver with reins in hand furiously lashing four large greyish white horses into a frenzy. He stood rooted to the spot for what seemed like an eternity (probably but a few seconds) and then turned on his heels and raced back the way he had come. He was scared out of his mind and found hidden strength to keep on running at high speed, expecting at any second the coach and horses to crash over him.

Eventually he arrived, without breath and with a pounding heart at his girl friend's house, and was more than a little relieved when the door was opened to his frantic knocking. Only then and not a moment before, did he turn around but there was no sign of any coach or horses. Needless to say, never again did he walk that stretch of road at night.

I was quite 'chilled' to discover that early this century a coach driver by the name of John Bowker and three of his team of four horses were killed on this road when they failed to negotiate a bend.

8.

Folklore

'Hen Fenyw Fach Cydweli' (The Old Maid of Kidwelly)
Another claim to fame by Kidwelly is that it is one of the few places
in Wales which figures in a popular Welsh Nursery Rhyme dedicated
to the town.

> Hen fenyw fach Cydweli
> Yn gwerthu losyn du
> Yn rhifo deg am ddime
> Ond un-ar-ddeg i mi.
> Wel! dyma'r newydd gore ddaeth i mi i mi
> Yn rhifo deg am ddime
> Ond un-ar-ddeg i mi.

This is a very old nursery rhyme and in English it would read:

> The old maid of Kidwelly
> A seller of sweets is she
> She is counting out ten for a halfpenny
> But always eleven for me.
> Well that is the best news that I ever did see
> She is counting out ten for a halfpenny
> But always eleven for me.

Most nursery rhymes, nonsense though they sound, have their foundation in some forgotten happening. However, no one knows who
the original old maid of Kidwelly was.

A delightful tale is told regarding the old maid of Kidwelly by
Showell Styles in *Welsh Walks and Legends of South Wales*, 1977:

The identity of the 'Old Maid of Kidwelly' is unknown but she
could have been the Lady Hawise de Londres.

The Lady Hawise was as good as she was beautiful, which is to
say a great deal. Throughout her childhood and youth she had lived
in the Norman Castle of Kidwelly, her father being Castellan who

held the fortress under King Henry III. Although she was of the purest Norman blood she had many friends among the Welsh folk in the village of Kidwelly and spoke their language as fluently as her own Norman-French. Kidwelly Castle was very much involved in the wars and politics of that unruly time, when Welsh princes alternately bargained with or fought against the rulers of England who sought to rule Wales. Indeed, when Hawise was a small girl the fortress was besieged and captured by a Welsh chieftain named Rhys Grug but she and her father, with a few of the garrison, escaped with their lives. This was in the year 1215 and for five years Rhys Grug held Kidwelly Castle. Then Llewellyn ap Iorwerth (called the great) became overlord of Wales and married King Henry's sister, the Princess Joan. He was responsible to the King of England for the maintenance of peace and order in his country. Llewellyn restored the castle to the De Londres family giving them a parchment declaring their possession under his 'overlordship'. Hawise came back to her home and her friends in Kidwelly.

But Wales still seethed with rebellion against the English sovereignty and in a skirmish with the rebels Hawise's father was killed. Shortly after this incident Meredydd ap Rhys, a high ranking Welshman who had sworn eternal enmity against all who had Norman blood in their veins, attacked Kidwelly Castle with a large force and succeeded in taking it despite a valiant defence. Once more Hawise escaped. She took refuge in a stronghold at Carmarthen where romance was kindled, for she married a noble knight named Patrick de Chatworth. Marriage did not entirely satisfy her however. Since she had no brothers she was the heiress of Kidwelly and it sorted neither with her pride nor with her affections that she should be dispossessed. She resolved to appeal to Prince Llewellyn who was then domiciled at Dryslwyn Castle with his wife Joan.

De Chatworth had been sorely wounded in a fight with outlaws and was being cared for by the monks at Whitland, so Hawise went to Dryslwyn alone. It was an unpropitious time to make an appeal to the Prince of Wales. Llewellyn had recently quarrelled with King Henry and was preparing to oppose him. At first he refused to listen to Hawise or take any notice of the deed of possession bearing his seal, which she had brought with her. But then the Princess interceded for her.

"Your honour will be impugned, my lord, if you repudiate this deed given under your hand," she told her husband.

The Prince frowned and considered. Hawise's demand was just;

but he needed Meredydd ap Rhys's help if he was to oppose the English king. Eventually he sent for his clerk, bade him write a message and attached his seal.

"This will content you, my Lady Hawise," he said, handing her a document. "It is my command to Ap Rhys to surrender Kidwelly Castle to yourself, when you shall give the parchment to him with your own hand."

He smiled into his beard as he said it. And when Hawise, who hurried at once to Kidwelly, reached the township she understood the meaning of his smile. She could not possibly go to the castle, the Welsh folk told her; Meredydd ap Rhys had sworn that any person of Norman blood who came within reach of his spearmen or range of his archers, would be slain instantly.

Hawise was not daunted, however. She sought out an old friend of hers, Angharad the seller of cakes and sweetmeats, who was by now a withered old maid who still plied her trade between village and castle. And next morning, dressed in Angharad's red cloak and the frilled linen hood that concealed her face, she shambled along with an old woman's bent and crouching gait, to the door of the castle. The spearmen on duty there let 'old Angharad' through with a jest and she went into the inner ward and the hall where Meredydd and his men-at-arms were breaking their fast. Hawise made a round of the lower benches with her basket of sweetmeats, croaking praise of her wares in Welsh to the men who sprawled there. Then she advanced to the dais where their lord sat and taking the parchment from her basket laid it before Meredydd, who gave a start when he saw the seal of his Prince and the words of unwelcome command. "Who are you?" he demanded, and glared at the woman before him.

Hawise straightened her body and threw back the hood. "I am the Lady Hawise," she said in Welsh, "rightful Castellan of Kidwelly – as your Prince's command will assure you."

Meredydd sprang to his feet with hand on hilt of dagger. Then he bowed his head.

"I would not retract what I have sworn for any man," he said. "But your courage and beauty, lady, have gained the day. By this time tomorrow I and my men will be gone and the castle will be yours."

So the Lady Hawise came into her own once more. And it is said that the chief lady in waiting at the Castle of Kidwelly was a little old maid named Angharad.

FOLK TALE

Giraldus Cambrensis allows us a glimpse into the private life of Maurice de Londres when he records that Maurice owned a forest in the neighbourhood of Kidwelly well stocked with animals which included a large herd of deer. He did everything in his power to protect them, and Giraldus relates to an episode in connection with Maurice's partiality to deer and his wife's partiality to sheep.

As is so often the case, Maurice's wife was only too well aware of her husband's affection for the deer and being somewhat irritated about the whole set-up decided to play a practical 'joke' on him. Adjacent to the forest and running down to the sea Maurice was also the owner of the broad pastureland upon which a massive flock of sheep grazed. His wife petulantly contrived a prank and persuaded the shepherds and the household servants to co-operate and assist with her plan.

Maurice was characteristically a simple soul and was very defensive of his possessions. His wife took advantage of his credulity and one day she turned to him and said – "It seems very odd to me that you own all these animals, yet you have no control whatsoever on them. The deer are altogether untrained and instead of responding to your bidding, it seems to me they are 'telling' you what to do! They run completely wild and there is just no limit to their depredations, and now they are savaging the sheep. Our flock was at one time so huge it was impossible to count them, and even now their number remains large enough but there has most certainly been a big reduction."

Later on, she had two stags cut open and the intestines padded with wool. Maurice was completely taken in by his wife's trickery and being totally unsuspicious, set his hounds to attack the deer.

AN ENCHANTED STREAM

Wales has been described as the land of wells, as hidden in its hills and crags more than a thousand in number to which some belief or legend is attached, have been noted and recorded – wishing wells, healing wells, haunted wells and countless stories of 'dirgelaidd dŵr' (mysterious waters).

Kemmis Buckley – an authority on Welsh wells declares – 'Pistyll Teilo' (the stream of St Teilo) is a wild and exceptionally melancholy ravine situated below the site of the old chapel dedicated to St Teilo, located to the south of the road leading from Mynydd-y-Garreg to Four Roads, and is well described in the words of the local  historian. "The path to the pistyll is extremely inaccessible and dangerous and one has to descend the rock face to reach it. The traditional saying from the past persists that one could get a draught fairer than wine here and that the stream had special powers. I remember twisting my feet as a young lad, and a surgical expert's advice to facilitate my recovery and free me from lameness, was to hold my feet under the main torrent of the gully."

Mr Ebenezer Jones of Bryn Forest, interviewed in his 86th year, remembers that miners believing the waters of the 'pistyll' could remove bruises incurred in their work, held their wounded limbs in the icy water until 'they were red hot'.

It is said that a ghost haunts this 'pistyll' and cries in pitiful tones: "Mae'n hir ac yn oer i aros i orwyr Wil Wattar", (It is long and cold and tiresome waiting for the descendants of Wil Wattar). To this very day, natives of the district would rather not walk at night-time along the road which skirts this ravine, and one can only assume that the reason is the ghostly voice which supposedly emanates from the bottom of the 'cwm' (valley). If it were possible to trace the identity of Wil Wattar, a whole wealth of local legend might be exposed.

Here are two such tales of the enchanted stream of St Teilo near Kidwelly:

1. To the south of the road from Mynydd-y-Garreg to Four Roads stands the ruins of an old chapel. There in a quiet ravine below the chapel flows the dark water of Pistyll Teilo (the stream of St Teilo).

Its healing powers were well known in the parish of Kidwelly and many folk came there to bathe their bruised and crooked limbs.

One day, two men – one with blue scars caused through working on the coal face, the other with a lameness – decided to test the magic properties of the 'pistyll'. They left the road and descended a rugged path in the rocks which led down to the ravine. When they reached the 'pistyll' they found it to be cool and silent there, although along the way skylarks had been singing in the afternoon sun. Now, there was only the faint sound of the water as it rippled by. They rolled their trouser legs up to their knees and chose a spot where the water ran deep. An odd sight they must have looked sitting together on the mossy bank beside the stream, with spindly legs dangling in the water. The 'pistyll' licked their limbs with an ice cold tongue. But steadfast they sat with wry faces until their ailing parts were blue and numb. After a while they were startled by a haunting sound. A voice like the whisper of waves on a distant shore, called to them. They looked around with wide staring eyes but there was no one to be seen. Then the voice came again, clearer this time – "it is cold and lonely waiting for the sons of William," it said in their native tongue. And echoes whispered back from the rocky ravine ". . . sons of William . . . sons of William." "Tylwyth Teg" (the little folk), muttered the lame man. But his companion well remembered the little folk's fear of water. "Ysbrydion!" (ghosts), he shouted.

Then quickly they gathered into their arms their bundles of boots and clothing and scrambled up the path to the roadway, where they arrived pale and breathless, with fresh bruises to heal.

2. It was getting dark when the old man passed the chapel ruins. He pulled on the reins and stopped for a while to give his horse a rest. Then he lit the lantern hanging beside him on the cart and climbed down to stretch his legs. He would be home before nightfall. His faithful collie loped off toward the old chapel with his nose to the ground.

Presently, the dog came slinking back; the horse made a whinnying sound and reared in the shafts. The old man, too, was strangely disturbed, for a voice was heard calling from the dusky light below the ruins. Like a sudden wind moaning through the ravine and then drifting away in the distance it sighed ". . . sons of William . . . of William . . . William . . ."

To this day, the folk of the district never pass along the road above the ravine after nightfall because they fear the ghostly voice which calls from the bottom of the 'cwm'. Perhaps one day the 'descendants of William' will be discovered and the mystery of the ghostly voice solved. And if ever they immerse their aching limbs in the chill waters of Pistyll Teilo the voice will be silent forever.

9.

Traditions

THE BLACK CAT

There is a tradition that Kidwelly was once deserted because of the plague which killed off most of its inhabitants. The survivors fled and when they returned after an interval, the only living creature they found was a cat, which from then on was used as Kidwelly's heraldic symbol. However, you must remember that this is 'folk lore' but many coats-of-arms are based on this kind of story and would be acceptable to heralds.

The seal has the following inscription:

SIGILLUM DE KIDWELLY COMMUN
(Seal of the Community [Borough] of Kidwelly).

ORIGIN OF THE NAME

The origin of the name 'Kidwelly' is shrouded in mystery. Variation in the way it was written in ancient documents such as Patent Rolls, Charter Rolls, Inquisition Post Mortem, does little to help unravel the puzzle. The distortions are in some instances almost unrecognisable. These are some of the examples – Kedwelly, Kadweli, Cadweli, Kedwelli, Kydwelly, Kydwelli, Kydwellye, Kidwelli, Kaddwelye, Kidwellie, Kidwelyn, Cetgueli and Cathgweli. English traveller and historian Leyland, writing in the 1540s, states "that the town derives the name from Cathweli or Cattalectus because Cattas used to make his bed in an oak tree there."

Many other suggestions have been put forward as to the origin of the name – one plausible theory comes from the Welsh form Cydweli – 'Cyd' a junction or joining and 'wyl' a flow or gushing out, with the town being situated near the junction of the Gwendraeth Fawr and Gwendraeth Fach where the two rivers flow together into the sea.

MEDIEVAL CUSTOMS

Survival of medieval customs in Kidwelly from the Tudor period to the beginning of the Industrial Revolution of the eighteenth century reflects the tremendous heritage of the area. I quote from *Local History and Folklore*, Charles Pythian Adams, 1975, who explains the ancient understanding of time and its close links with Agriculture:

> "To appreciate the medieval understanding of time one must bear in mind that although some churches were boasting clocks from the 14th century – the days and hence the hours varied in their length from winter to summer according to the light. It is probably more accurate in fact to characterise the medieval understanding of time as determined by temporal blocks – quarters, seasons or holidays. That this was due in large part to the demands of agriculture, its busy times and otherwise, is undisputable. It is evident that many popular festivals, such as Plough Monday, were often closely associated with either the beginning or the end of an important farming process. Michaelmas ushered in a season of winter sowing, slaughter, threshing and winnowing; Christmas, spring plough-ing and sowing; Lady Day, fallow ploughing and shearing; and Midsummer the harvesting of hay and corn.
>
> "In the Celtic areas the year was bisected in early Novem-ber and at May Day. If the former marked the beginning of winter and hence the winter quartering of stock, May Day may well have signalised the moment to put the stock to summer pasturage."

'Calan Mai'   May Day – the Festival of Summer and the recurring cycle of rebirth and regrowth.

'Calan Gaeaf'   November 1st – commencement of the Winter cycle.

These two dates were pivots of the Welsh year and were im-portant in Welsh social life, but the introduction of the Christian calendar brought in new beliefs and practices, especially festivals, notably Christmas and Easter. Ancient celebrations took place in Kidwelly well into the nineteenth century at Christmas, Easter, May Day and 1st November, the latter date being known as 'Diwrnod

Rhana' (Thanksgiving Day). Some of the ancient customs which can
be traced in the town include:

'Plygain'	–	Before cock crow
'Mawrth Ynyd'	–	Shrove Tuesday
'Gŵyl Fair Canhwylle'	–	Mary's Festival of Candles
'Calan Mai'	–	May Day
'Y Fedwen'	–	The May Pole
'Diwrnod Rhana'	–	Thanksgiving Day

plus the very many associated with 'Dydd Calan' (New Year's Day),
i.e.:

'Dŵr Newydd'	–	New Water
'Mari Lwyd"	–	Holy Mary or the Old Grey Mare
'Y Berllan gyda Rhigymau'	–	The Orchard with Rhymes
'Calennig'	–	New Year's Gift
'Whipo'r Celyn'	–	Holly Beating.

One other tradition that can be traced way back is a great fair
held on St Mary Magdalen's Day, which dates from the thirteenth
century.

The preservation of so many of these old customs in and around
Kidwelly to such a recent date as the middle of the last century
raises the question as to why?

It might be expected that the customs referred to would have
become extinct much earlier in a borough of the importance and
position of Kidwelly, than in comparatively isolated inland towns.
However, this was not the case and the customs, especially those of
ecclesiastical sanction, disappeared in country parishes like Llandyfaelog and Llangyndeyrn. Further, it is generally held that the
forces which gradually drove out these medieval beliefs and customs received a more ready welcome in towns where there was a
marked English element than in those parts of the country where
Welsh sympathies were strongest. Evidence suggests from the parish
registers of Kidwelly during this period that a large percentage of
the inhabitants were English, or at any rate of English parentage.

The customs suggest that at an earlier period medieval influences
were very powerful in Kidwelly and at a later period certain conditions prevailed which intensified the conservative spirit of the

inhabitants. Could the answer be in the fact that from the sixteenth century Kidwelly was for some reason or other isolated from the larger life of the world beyond. There was no infusion of new blood; there was apparently little intercourse with neighbouring towns. Thus the economic condition of Kidwelly tended to intensify the conservatism of the town inhabitants, and there is no conservatism to be compared with that of a small town whose glory has departed. Curiously, the town was among the first in Wales to respond to the awakening influences of the Industrial Revolution of the 18th century.

This section of the book draws heavily on *Carmarthenshire Gleanings*, written by Rev. Gruffydd Evans, published in 1915.

'Plygain' (Early Dawn)

An important festival at Christmas in Wales was the 'Plygain' which means before cock crow. The 'Plygain' was a religious service held in the Parish Church at three o'clock on Christmas morning, to watch the dawn, to commemorate the coming of Christ and the daybreak of Christianity. The service comprised song, prayer, praise and thanksgiving, and there was at that early hour a large congregation, even in remote districts. Many came from long distances – often three or four miles – on a frosty night or through snow. In the course of time the hour was changed from three to four or five, and such services were held in Kidwelly well into the early part of this century. At a service held early this century, 'Plygain' began at five o'clock in St Mary's Parish Church. All worshippers carried candles decorated with ribbons or streamers of coloured paper. These candles were of various colours and after the service and carol singing was ended, the candles were put out and left for the use of the Church. It was deemed most improper to present any but the best wax candles – a detail which reflects the medieval and ceremonial origin of the custom. 'Plygain' is still celebrated in some country parishes.

There were two ancient customs celebrated in the town associated with Lent:

'Mawrth Ynyd' (Shrove Tuesday)

Two of the most unique observances in this area were associated with 'Mawrth Ynyd' (Shrove Tuesday). The rites which are described here were celebrated on the eve of Ash Wednesday, that is the evening of Shrove Tuesday.

After dark, a number of youths would visit a house, or usually a farm in the locality, secretly place on the kitchen window sill what was called a 'Crochion Crewys' – either an eggshell or a scooped out turnip, containing little bits of bread, salt, leek, cabbage or some other vegetable, then recite rapidly and vigorously the following 'rhigwm' (rhyme), or a variant of it:

> "Crochion Crewys ar ben ffenest
> Bara, halen, cawl ceninen
> Os na ddaw nôl cyn Nos Lun Pasg
> Cant Punt o fine."

> "Lenten crock on the window sill
> Bread, salt, leek broth
> If it will not be back before Easter Monday evening
> A fine of a hundred pounds."

The kitchen door would open suddenly and members of the household would rush out to try and capture the visitors. If one was caught, he was bound by the rules of the game, to clean and shine all the best boots in the house. Upon completion of this task he was rewarded with a generous helping of pancakes. The custom was exceedingly popular, and visits were not confined to farms. One person remembered the 'Crochion Crewys' placed on the window sill of his grandmother's house – the New Inn in Lady Street, Kidwelly.

Another custom was very popular in the town just over a hundred years ago – on the evening of Shrove Tuesday the youths made a collection of old tins and pans and kicked them with 'hideous-din' along the streets and even into houses if doors were inadvertently left open. In time this practice led to so much hooliganism that the police were called in. In origin, this rite undoubtedly belongs in the same category of events as the 'Crochion Crewys'. The 'Crochon' emphasized the nature of the fares to be eaten during Lent, the destruction of the pans emphasized the duty of putting away those cooking utensils which were associated with the more cheerful fare not lawful during the fast.

Both these customs originated in the Middle Ages and were obviously connected with the fasting of lent. There must have been quite a number of people who failed to fast and this practice was a stern warning to them.

'Gŵyl Fair y Canhwylle' (Mary's Festival of Candles)
An ancient custom in Kidwelly was the celebration of
the Feast of Purification (February 2nd) Candlemas. In
the gradual change from winter to spring the feast of
Candlemas formerly held an important role. To quote
the Rev. Gruffydd Evans, *Carmarthenshire Gleanings*: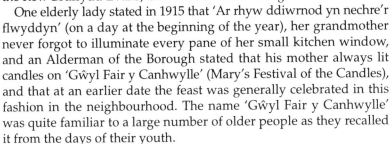

One elderly lady stated in 1915 that 'Ar rhyw ddiwrnod yn nechre'r
flwyddyn' (on a day at the beginning of the year), her grandmother
never forgot to illuminate every pane of her small kitchen window,
and an Alderman of the Borough stated that his mother always lit
candles on 'Gŵyl Fair y Canhwylle' (Mary's Festival of the Candles),
and that at an earlier date the feast was generally celebrated in this
fashion in the neighbourhood. The name 'Gŵyl Fair y Canhwylle'
was quite familiar to a large number of older people as they recalled
it from the days of their youth.

Some time in the autumn, the mistress of a farm ceremoniously
gave 'Y forwyn fawr' (the head maid) a lighted candle for use in the
outhouses. According to rule the maid was bound to hand the
candle back to her mistress on 'Gŵyl Fair y Canhwylle'. The older
folk were positive about the date on which the candle had to be
brought back. It was considered that on February 2nd, artificial
light could be dispensed with. One Kidwelly gentleman was once
reprimanded with these significant words: "Mae Gŵyl Fair y Canhwylle wedi dod, dylech feedo'r creduried cyn fod eisiau lamp
arnoch chi." (Candlemas has arrived, you ought to feed the animals
before a lamp is required).

'Calan Mai' (May Day)
At one time, this day 'Calan Mai' (May Day) was a great day in
Kidwelly. To quote the Rev. Gruffydd Evans, *Carmarthenshire Gleanings*, writing in 1915: "Most of the old folk consulted, knew of the
practice of placing branches of mountain ash over the doors and
windows on the Calends of May. One of them remarked that he saw
doors and windows garnished in the town of Kidwelly as late as
1845 – 'hen gwstwm oedd e' (it was an old custom) said one; 'cadw
gofid mas o'r tŷ' (to keep trouble out of the house) said another. The
majority, however, said that the object was to keep out the
witches who were mischievously active on the first day of
May. One person maintained that holly as well as mountain
ash was used in the decorations, the explanation being
– 'mae ofon y celyn ar y gwiddon, mae'n eu pigo nhw'
(the witches are afraid of the holly, it pricks them.')."

The practice of hanging branches of hawthorn or green birch outside the doors and houses and cattle stalls as a protection against witches goes back to the sixteenth century, whilst mountain ash was still held to possess the same protective quality in some areas as late as the nineteenth century.

'Y Fedwen' (The May Pole)
'Y Fedwen' (The May Pole) also marked the festivities of 'Calan Mai' (May Day) in Kidwelly. In South Wales the custom was called 'Codi'r Fedwen' (Raising the Birch). The May Pole was prepared by painting it in different colours; then the leader of the dance would come and place his circle of ribbon around the pole, and each in his turn after him until the May Pole was beribboned from one end to the other. It was described by one who saw the festivities as "a pole about 12 to 14 feet in length, made gay with evergreens, flowers and ribbons, was carried by the young people along the main streets of the borough with a great deal of singing and merriment." The procession would return to a spot within the Barbican walls where the old Castle School now stands. The pole was fixed into the ground and dancing around it was kept up until evening.

'Diwrnod Rhana' (Thanksgiving Day)
Another old custom of religious origin was carried out at Hallowmass, a tradition which in the minds of the people had completely lost its original significance, and had become bound up with the harvest. The verse recited on the occasion, however, proves beyond all doubt the true origin of the custom. The day was called 'Diwrnod Rhana' (Thanksgiving Day) and the 'rhana' took place 'y dydd cyn Ffair Glangaeaf' (the day before the Feast of All Saints) known as Hallowmass which is observed on 1st November and regarded as winter's eve. One of the Welsh names for Hallowmass is 'Dygwyl yr eneidiau'.

The evening preceding 'Diwrnod Rhana' (Thanksgiving Day), the good wife of the farm busied herself with baking large flat cakes. Early next day, women and children of the labouring class came to the kitchen door reciting:

"Rhana! Rhana! Dwgwl Aneide
    Rhan i nhad am gwyiro scidie

Rhan i mam am gwyiro sane
Rhan i'r plant sy'n aros gartre."

"Share out! Share out! on All Souls Day
A portion to father for cobbling our shoes
A portion to mother for darning our socks
A portion to the children who are staying at home.

The good wife then asked 'Faint ych chi?' (How many are you?)
and distributed the cakes according to the number in the family.

The gifts were not bestowed indiscriminately in Kidwelly. Only
those who had helped, or the children of those who had helped at
the harvest got the 'Pice Rhana' (Soul Cakes) as they were called.
Thus in the course of time the custom became associated with the
harvest.

There were many ancient practices in Kidwelly connected with
'Dydd Calan' (New Year's Day) as follows: 'Dŵr Newydd' (Fresh
Water), 'Mari Lwyd' (Holy Mary, or The Old Grey Mare), 'Y Berllan'
(The Orchard), 'Calennig' (New Year's Gift) and 'Whipo'r Celyn'
(Holly Beating).

'Dŵr Newydd' (Fresh Water)
The custom of New Year's Water, recorded principally in South
Wales, appears to have disappeared round about the turn of the
century. Early on New Year's morning crowds of boys visited houses
in the neighbourhood carrying with them a vessel containing cold
spring water, freshly drawn that very morning, with a twig of
boxwood, holly, myrtle or other evergreen. The hands and faces of
every person they met on their rounds were sprinkled with water in
return for a copper or two. Each room in every house they entered
would be sprinkled with New Year's Water and the residents who
would often still be in bed were wished a Happy New Year.

With a sprig of boxwood, mothers would sprinkle fresh water on
the faces of their sleeping children. It is recorded that at an address
in Lady Street, Kidwelly, this custom was being practised as late as
New Year's Day 1913.

'Mari Lwyd' (Holy Mary or The Old Grey Mare)
Another old custom – the 'Mari Lwyd' (Holy Mary) held on New
Year's Day was immensely popular in the Kidwelly district. A good
description of the 'Mari Lwyd' is given by Trefor M. Owen in *Welsh
Folk Customs*, I quote:

"The 'Mari Lwyd' itself consisted of a horse's skull. The lower jaw was fixed with a spring which caused it to shut with a loud snap when operated by the person carrying it. A pole about five feet in length was inserted into the horse skull and a white sheet draped over it. Coloured ribbons were used to decorate the skull and bottle glass was used to represent the eyes; a piece of black cloth was sewn onto the sheet to serve as ears. The man carrying the 'Mari' stood underneath the sheet holding the pole and operated the lower jaw with a short wooden handle. Reins with bells attached were placed on the Man's head and held by the leader who also carried a stick for knocking on doors. When the procession approached a house it intended to visit, the leader tapped the door while the party sang traditional rhymes."

The 'Mari Lwyd' and her friends would then be invited in for food and drinks.

'Y Berllan gyda Rhigymau' (The Orchard with Rhymes)

A very interesting Welsh calendar custom associated with twelfth night was wassailing. The custom in Kidwelly as part of the wassail ceremony was called 'Y Berllan' (The Orchard). In this area the 'Berllan' was a small rectangular board with a circle marked in the centre and ribs of wood running from this point to each of the four angles. An apple was attached to each corner of the board, and within the circle a tree with a miniature bird thereon!

The 'Berllan' was taken round the area on New Year's Day by a group of young men. One of the group who approached the house chosen to be honoured by their visit, carried the 'Berllan'. Another carried 'a large cup full of beer' – in fact a wassail bowl – and yet another carried a candle to burn out the Old Year and light in the New Year.

The song which accompanied the 'Berllan' ceremony included in it:

"A chyda ni mae perllan, a dryw bach ynddi'n hedfan
Rheolwr pob adar yw hwnnw."

(And with us we have a Perllan, with a little wren flying in it
He is the ruler of all birds).

The 'Berllan' in Kidwelly existed alongside the 'Mari Lwyd' (Holy Mary) and both were performed on New Year's Day.

'Calennig' (New Year's Gift)
Presenting gifts on New Year's Day is an ancient custom, once widely observed but now displaced by the growing importance of Christmas and Christmas presents. At one time, New Year's Day remained in Welsh culture, as is in Scotland, of more importance than Christmas Day.

In Wales, 'Calennig' (gifts) were associated with New Year's Day. The practice of collecting the 'Calennig' was observed principally by children and was carried out from the stroke of midnight until noon on New Year's Day.

I quote Iorwerth C. Peate writing on *Tradition & Folk Life in Wales*:

"I well remember parties of 4 or 8 young people singing 'Y Bwthyn ar a Bryn' (The Cottage on the Hill) and other Victorian airs outside our house about 2 or 3 o'clock in the morning, and my father rewarding them with sixpenny pieces dropped from the bedroom window. Later in the morning, the small children came singing simple rhymes. The practice ceased at mid-day."

'Whipo'r Celyn' (Holly Beating)
Another ancient custom 'Whipo'r Celyn' (Holly Beating) had degenerated into a barbarous tradition. If a girl or even a married woman was caught out of doors on 'bore Dydd Calan' (the morning of New Year's Day) groups of men and boys armed with large bushes of prickly holly would set upon her. They would proceed to thrash her naked and unprotected arms 'nes fo'r gwaed yn dod' (until blood was drawn). Instances were known where participants in this unholy rite actually entered homes and dragged out their victims.

OLD FUNERAL CUSTOMS IN KIDWELLY

Tradition was very carefully observed on the day of a funeral; two bells tolled at 2 o'clock. The road in front of the house was swept clean and generally sprinkled with sand and laurel leaves. The older people talked extensively about the funeral custom in the upper classes in the mid-19th century. All those invited to the funeral stood reverently at the door of the house. A woman would bring out a large pewter dish laden with rosemary and would present each of the mourners with a sprig to be carried in the procession and then thrown into the grave. Another tray followed, laden with cakes, and then a special cup called 'Ebilon', filled with elderberry wine. Each person in turn took a little cake and then sipped a little of the wine.

THE WELL CULT

The faith and belief in wells from the earliest times is highlighted by Dr. Hartwell Jones, *Celtic Britain and the Pilgrim Movement*. I quote:

> "The underlying principle of water worship is readily recognisable. Water was beneficial – it afforded refreshment and invigorated the human body when fatigued. Growth and life flourished on the banks of rivers and showers of rain renewed fertility and revived the face of the earth. Some wells possessed medicinal values and attracted masses of people because they accommodated the physical and spiritual needs of so many. Added to these attractions was the fact that water was an important element in family life, not only as a means of sustenance but also for use in religious ceremonies. It was just a short step therefore to the deification of the spring. In Christian lore, the method usually adopted for producing wells was by the stroke of a saint's staff, hand or foot on a suitable or qualifying site. The choice of seasons for periodic pilgrimages to wells is not devoid of significance, and is proof that the custom dates back to the cult of the pagan. These expeditions were made in the spring when the ice had melted, and at midsummer when nature was in full bloom, for this was the time when the 'divine powers' especially demanded homage."

Wales has often been described as a 'land of wells', there being literally thousands hidden amongst its hills. There were 'holy wells', 'healing wells' and many more were merely 'wishing wells', but they were all regarded as places of magic and mystery. Early beliefs and superstitions maintained many customs and rituals connected with wells. People would drink the water and then throw pins into the well for good luck, and in other instances those with a desire for good health would wash themselves in water drawn from the well. They believed that some wells held special healing powers for all known physical diseases, whilst others held special powers to bring good fortune. These superstitions were taken very seriously and folk would travel great distances to visit a well, in search of a cure for an ailment, or in the hope of bringing about a change in luck or prosperity.

From time immemorial, in Wales and elsewhere, well springs were closely connected with religious observances. Parishes dedicated to the Virgin Mary generally had a Ffynnon Fair (St Mary's Well). These wells were considered sacrosanct and the waters were said to be purer than waters of other wells. Kidwelly had a Ffynnon Fair located near the castle and according to an old legend there was a tragic tale connected with it. I quote from *Haunted Britain*, written by Anthony Hippisley Coxe:

"In a marshy field 300 yards north of the castle, surrounded by a circle of stones, stands Ffynnon Fair, where the Virgin Mary is said to have been killed. According to this apocryphal story she came by ship and was murdered, and where she fell a spring rose."

The author continues and writes about Priddy in Somerset:

"Perhaps she came to visit places where Christ is said to have spent part of the 'lost years' – that period of his life between the ages of 12 and 30 about which nothing is known. People may wonder why there is no evidence of His visit, but it is possible that many young men came here with traders from the eastern Mediterranean. I have found quite a number of people who believe that Joseph of Arimathea was a tin trader who visited Cornish mines between AD 13 and 30, and brought Jesus with him."

According to another local tradition in connection with this dubious old legend, the man who slew the Virgin Mary was accursed, as was his family, and his descendants are marked out to this day as people who never succeed in any kind of undertaking they pursue. This is an old tale and one could ask why this particular well and why the story associated with it is not better known. Could it be that the answer lies perhaps in the fact that in past generations, the inhabitants of Kidwelly were not too anxious to admit that their forbears had carried out such an evil and shameful deed.

It was customary to add brown sugar to well water before drinking it and this practice seems to have been more prevalent in the Kidwelly district than anywhere else in the whole of Carmarthenshire. One obvious reason was that the sugar disguised the metallic taste of water which contains mineral substances. Nevertheless, the waters of Ffynnon Stockwell which tasted perfectly pure, were subject to this tradition, and indeed in the case of Ffynnon Stockwell, special mugs were kept solely for this purpose. On Palm Sunday in particular, parents would place brown sugar into these mugs and take their children to the well where they would dilute the sugar in the well water and drink the syrup. A rendezvous at this well took place as recently as Palm Sunday 1911. It is interesting and noteworthy that this old custom was so popular at a Festival of the Christian Church.

There was another Ffynnon Fair in the district, at Tyhir Farm in Mynydd-y-Garreg – both were holy wells. In Kidwelly it was a special custom to visit holy wells at Easter. The best known wells in addition to the two Ffynnon Fairs were Ffynnon Sul, Ffynnon Cadwgan situated near the Gletwyn Farm, Ffynnon Fihangel in Parc Shon Edwards near Muddlescwm Farm, Ffynnon Cobswell near the Arlish, Ffynnon Stockwell and Pistyll Teilo in Mynydd-y-Garreg. Most of the holy wells and indeed some of the others, were renowned for their medicinal values. Pistyll Teilo, situated near Capel Teilo in Mynydd-y-Garreg, was a favourite resort of folk suffering from sprains and similar complaints. It was said that a ghost formerly haunted this spot and that natives of the district would not walk at night time along the road which skirts the ravine.

Ffynnon Fihangel (St Michael's Well)
In a small well chamber on Parc Shon Edward, Kidwelly in the Parish of St Mary – formerly a popular resort on Palm Sunday. Not far away stood the medieval chapel of St Michael – (Seynt Mighell is Chappel within the foreignry of Kidwelly 1505).

(Extracted from an old document.)

Ffynnon Sul
Remembered within living memory as a spring that flowed into a well at the foot of the rising ground behind Kidwelly Castle. The hill was called 'Mons Solomon' in an ancient grant, and in 1779 a Kidwelly Rent Roll mentions a field called 'Parc Ffynnon Sul, the water now supplies the town'. Traditionally it is said that a prince named Benisel was slain here, and a well sprang up marking the spot where he was killed. Local inhabitants resorted to this well for the purpose of drinking its waters from the most ancient of times. There appears to have been an old superstition that upon drinking the water and dropping a key or pin into it, the fairy goddess of the well would bring good luck and good health. The custom was observed on Easter Sunday when people would congregate en masse at the well to participate in the legendary ritual.

There were other substantially documented wells in the parish named as follows:

St Ellen's Well situated near Frogmor Street – documented in the year 1415.

Ffynnon-y-Pistyll – on land called Pistyll near the town – reputed to cure sore eyes.

Ffynnon Dewi (St David's Well) situated probably near the churchyard.

Ffynnon Cwm Hed – located near Muddlescwm.

Ffynnon Diana – so called by reason it was the name of the woman who lived in a nearby cottage (located near Waungadog).

Ffynnon yr Alderman – located near The Mill.

Ffynnon y Gongell – established now in the bed of the Gwendraeth Fach above the old tin works.

Ffynnon Dan-y-Gaer – situated at Pantglas Farm.

Ffynnon Shon Hugh.

Saunders Well.

Stewards Well – which was to be found on the route leading to Carmarthen (possibly Rogerley Farm).

Many of these wells, for a variety of reasons (e.g. purity, cold temperature, healing properties) attracted people right up to the beginning of the present century.

Night of Kidwelly 'Hiring Fair'
(Photograph: 'W. H. Morris Collection)

ANCIENT FAIRS

The antiquity of most of the existing fairs is beyond measure but there are those who own records which prove their age. The Charter of the Borough of Kidwelly (granted in 1619 during the reign of James I) quotes thus – "3 Fairs are now holden and kept from time whof the memy of man is not to contry are accustomed to have been holden and kept yrly in divers sevl places – (i.e.) one within the walls of the sd Boro on the feast of St Mary Magdalen, another at Llangendeirne within 3 miles of the sd Boro and within the circuits and liberties thof upon the feast of St James the Apostle and the 3rd within the walls of the sd Boro upon the feast of St Luke the Evangelist."

The Rev. Gruffydd Evans, *Carmarthen Gleanings*, 1915, comments on two points of interest:

"Strangely enough the most popular fair in Kidwelly is not held on 'Gŵyl Fair' the festival of St Mary but on St Luke's Day, hence 'Ffair Gŵyl Lug'. An elderly lady who was brought up in the neighbourhood of Llansaint near Kidwelly, remarked that everybody went to the fair. 'Nid oedd y llaeth yn cael i hilo i'r pedyll ar fore Gŵyl Lug; yr oedd e yn cael i roi i gyd i'r plant'. (The milk was not strained into pans on St Luke's morn; it was all given to the children.) That the chief fair should be held on St Luke's Day is somewhat anomalous, for the fine old parish church is dedicated to the Virgin, one of the principal thoroughfares is known as our Lady Street and there were two holy wells in the parish named after St Mary. The other fair was the one held on St Mary Magdalen's Day, and the privilege of holding it was granted to Payn de Chaworth in the thirteenth century. That the Feast of St Magdalen and not one of the festivals dedicated to St Mary the Virgin, should be selected for the earliest fair referred to in the documents, is another perplexing problem upon which no light can be thrown."

As far back in the annals of time as 1280 and for many years thereafter there was a great eight day fair held at Kidwelly where bull and badger baiting and other cruel sports were extensively indulged in. The bullring was situated somewhere in Causeway Street near the entrance to St Mary's Church. A market was also held here twice a week. One of these ancient fairs continues to take place on October 29th (St Luke's Fair). At one time this fair was ranked one of the biggest in Wales and people came from far and wide to attend. It was common practice right up to the early part of this century to hire farm servants on six monthly or yearly engagements, beginning either May Day or on 1st November. Hiring fairs were held in many parts of Wales on or near these days. Many fairs were established to market cattle, sheep and pigs, but numerous other stalls would be added to sell clothes, boots, dishes etc.

Alwyn D. Rees sets the scene in *Life in a Welsh Countryside*:

"Itinerant traders and entertainers attended these festivals, bringing new fashions in wares and entertainment, thus making the occasion a point of contact with the outside world. In addition to the auctions and stock sales – which are the major attractions for men – there were street stalls selling a variety of merchandise, such as clothing and china, and a pleasure fair which attracted everybody. For many the main enjoyment would be found in walking to and fro on the heavily crowded roadway or simply chatting in little groups. Mostly young people participated in the celebrations, but there were many older people too and some of them remained until after midnight. The crowded road had an atmosphere comparable with that of a dance or large party. Old acquaintances were renewed and coming across friends and neighbours at the fair was part of the fun.

For the young men the opportunity of meeting girls from other districts was a major attraction. They were specially groomed for the occasion, and the girls smartly dressed. Small parties of each sex would move about accosting one another and forming little conversational groups. Later at night there was usually a fight or two between men from different districts – usually they fought over girls."

Four fairs continued to be held in Kidwelly in the early part of this century:

May Fair	–	First Tuesday after 20th May – horses, cattle and pigs.
August Fair	–	Held on 3rd and 4th of the month with cattle on the first day and pigs on the second day.
St Luke's Fair	–	October 29th – this was the hiring fair – 2 days.
Gwenllian Fair	–	First Monday in December – cattle and pigs.

Some of the older residents of the district can recall fairs with horses and cattle being sold on the first day and the second day was a pig fair, when Bridge Street and Lady Street were crammed with rows of carts full of pigs for sale. In those days a large number of the inhabitants reared pigs which were housed in pigsties sited at the bottom of the garden. A familiar scene would have been a salted pig cut up and hanging from the kitchen ceiling or larder. Others recall that farm servants were paid twice a year only, and as fair time was one of these 'high' days, the event was even more eagerly awaited, as picking up six months wages enabled them to really enjoy themselves. Those days are long gone and the pleasure fairs have lost the element of merriment, the shining steam engine has gone, as has the beautiful melodious organ and the old suspended swinging gondolas.

Bibliography

A History of Carmarthenshire – Sir John E. Lloyd. William Lewis Printers, 1939.

An Inventory of Ancient Monuments in Wales and Monmouthshire, Vol. V., H.M. Stationery Office London, 1917.

Black's Guide to North and South Wales, 1851.

Celtic Britain and the Pilgrim Movement – Dr Hartwell Jones. Hon. Society of Cymmrodorion, 1912.

Folklore of West and Mid Wales – Jonathan Caredig Davies. Llanerch Publishers, 1911.

Haunted Britain – Anthony Hippisley Coxe. Hutchinson & Co. Ltd., 1973.

History of Kidwelly – Rev. D. Daven Jones. W. Spurrell & Son, 1908.

Kidwelly Castle – C. A. Radleigh Radford. H.M. Stationery Office, 1933.

Kidwelly Tin Plate Works – A History – W. H. Morris, Llanelli Borough Council.

Legends and Folklore of South Wales – Hilda A. E. Roberts. Collins Press, 1931.

Life in a Welsh Countryside – Alwyn D. Rees. University of Wales Press, 1975.

Local History and Folklore – Charles Phythian Adams. Bedford Square Press, 1975.

Looking Around Llanelli – Harry Davies. Llanelli Town Council, 1985.

Rambles and Studies in Old South Wales – Wirt Sykes. Sampson Low, Marston, Searle & Rivington, 1881.

Tales of South Wales – Ken Radford. Skilton & Shaw Ltd., 1979.

The Gwendraeth Valleys Railway – M. C. R. Price. Oakwood Press, 1997.

The Holy Wells of Wales – Francis Jones. University of Wales Press, 1954.

The Itinerary Through Wales – Giraldus Cambrensis – Ernest Rhys. J. N. Dent & Co., London, 1908.

The Story of Carmarthenshire, II – A. G. Prys Jones. Christopher Davies, 1959.

Tradition and Folk Life – A Welsh View – Iorwerth C. Peate. Faber & Faber Ltd., 1972.

Welsh Folk Customs – Trevor M. Owen. Gomer Press, 1959.

Welsh Legends and Fairy Lore – D. Parry Jones. B. T. Batsford Ltd., 1953.

Welsh Smugglers – K. C. Watkins. James Pike Ltd., 1975.

Welsh Walks and Legends – South Wales – Showell Styles. John Jones Ltd., 1977.

'Carmarthenshire Gleanings', *Y Cymmrodor*, Vol. XXV – Rev. Gruffydd Evans, 1915.

'A Kidwelly Town Rental of the Early 16th Century', *Carmarthenshire Antiquary* – W. H. Morris. V. C. Lodwick & Sons, 1975.

'Canals of the Gwendraeth Valley', *Carmarthenshire Antiquary* – W. H. Morris.

Priory Church of St Mary's – Booklet.

Some Holy Wells of South Carmarthenshire – A Paper by Kemmis Buckley.

Transactions of the Carmarthenshire Antiquarian Society – Volumes I, II, IV, XIII, and XIV.

Wm. Hill Morris Collection – Carmarthen Record Office.

Llanelly Guardian, Llanelly Mercury, Carmarthen Journal.

The author has made every effort to contact copyright holders, but wishes to apologise to those he has been unable to trace.

Kidwelly Castle & St Marys Church